ROUTLEDGE LIBRARY EDITIONS:
PSYCHOLOGY OF EDUCATION

Volume 16

MODERN EDUCATIONAL PSYCHOLOGY

MODERN EDUCATIONAL PSYCHOLOGY

An historical introduction

E. G. S. EVANS

LONDON AND NEW YORK

First published in 1969 by Routledge & Kegan Paul Ltd

This edition first published in 2018
by Routledge
2 Park Square, Milton Park, Abingdon, Oxon OX14 4RN

and by Routledge
711 Third Avenue, New York, NY 10017

Routledge is an imprint of the Taylor & Francis Group, an informa business

© 1969 E. G. S. Evans

All rights reserved. No part of this book may be reprinted or reproduced or utilised in any form or by any electronic, mechanical, or other means, now known or hereafter invented, including photocopying and recording, or in any information storage or retrieval system, without permission in writing from the publishers.

Trademark notice: Product or corporate names may be trademarks or registered trademarks, and are used only for identification and explanation without intent to infringe.

British Library Cataloguing in Publication Data
A catalogue record for this book is available from the British Library

ISBN: 978-1-138-24157-2 (Set)
ISBN: 978-1-315-10703-5 (Set) (ebk)
ISBN: 978-1-138-06068-5 (Volume 16) (hbk)
ISBN: 978-1-138-06072-2 (Volume 16) (pbk)
ISBN: 978-1-315-16295-9 (Volume 16) (ebk)

Publisher's Note
The publisher has gone to great lengths to ensure the quality of this reprint but points out that some imperfections in the original copies may be apparent.

Disclaimer
The publisher has made every effort to trace copyright holders and would welcome correspondence from those they have been unable to trace.

Modern educational psychology
An historical introduction

by E. G. S. Evans
Institute of Education,
University of Southampton

LONDON
ROUTLEDGE & KEGAN PAUL
NEW YORK: HUMANITIES PRESS

*First published 1969
by Routledge & Kegan Paul Ltd
Broadway House, 68-74 Carter Lane
London, E.C.4*

*Printed in Great Britain
by Northumberland Press Limited
Gateshead*

© *E. G. S. Evans 1969*

*No part of this book may be reproduced
in any form without permission from
the publisher, except for the quotation
of brief passages in criticism*

*SBN 7100 6514 0 (c)
SBN 7100 6515 9 (p)*

THE STUDENTS' LIBRARY OF EDUCATION has been designed to meet the needs of students of Education at Colleges of Education and at University Institutes and Departments. It will also be valuable for practising teachers and educationists. The series takes full account of the latest developments in teacher-training and of new methods and approaches in education. Separate volumes will provide authoritative and up-to-date accounts of the topics within the major fields of sociology, philosophy and history of education, educational psychology, and method. Care has been taken that specialist topics are treated lucidly and usefully for the non-specialist reader. Altogether, the Students' Library of Education will provide a comprehensive introduction and guide to anyone concerned with the study of education and with educational theory and practice.

J. W. TIBBLE

The volume of new work each year in psychology which may have relevance to education—whether all such work is to be regarded as advancing the subject is a separate issue—is now very great indeed. The problem of teaching the subject to students of education becomes thereby increasingly difficult to solve, and when it comes to a principle of exclusion, the history of the subject is always in danger of being the victim.

Where this happens students are deprived of an opportunity to try to understand the evolution of ideas in the subject, and it is then at least doubtful whether they have much chance of fully understanding modern work. This is one reason for welcoming Dr. Evans' book. It is a lucid account within a brief compass of the main lines of thought which are still influential. Moreover the author has given sufficient references to enable students to follow up their own interests whether historical or contemporary, and there is no doubt that it should prove a most useful introductory source book for all students of education.

School of Education, BEN MORRIS
University of Bristol
28th April 1969

Contents

		page	
	Preface	page	ix
1	Child development		1
	Introduction		1
	Precursors		2
	Jean-Jacques Rousseau (1712-1778)		2
	Johann Heinrich Pestalozzi (1746-1827)		6
	Friedrich Froebel (1783-1852)		12
	The influence of Evolutionism		14
	Charles Darwin (1809-1882)		14
	Herbert Spencer (1820-1903)		15
	Systematic studies of children		17
	James Sully (1842-1923)		18
	Susan Isaacs (1885-1948)		18
	Arnold Gesell (1880-1961)		20
	John Brodus Watson (1878-1958)		22
	Jean Piaget (1896-)		25
	Summary		31
2	Theories of personality formation		33
	Introduction		33
	Depth or psychoanalytic theory		34

CONTENTS

	Social-field theories	38
	Instinct theory	41
	Allport's theory of functional autonomy	46
	Factoral or structural theories	49
	Conclusions	53
3	The psychology of learning	56
	Associationism	57
	Evolutionism	62
	Ebbinghaus's memory experiments	63
	Neurological and physiological studies	65
	Thorndike's animal experiments	66
	Watson and Behaviourism	71
	Learning by insight	75
4	Mental testing and measurement	81
	Early interest in the classification of the feeble-minded	81
	The influence of the early experimental psychologists	83
	The contributions of Sir Francis Galton	84
	Cattell and other early mental tests	86
	Binet and the rise of intelligence tests	86
	Group tests	90
	Theories of mental structure	92
	Spearman's two-factor theory	93
	Thomson's sampling theory	94
	Burt's theory of hierarchical structure	95
	Thurstone's primary mental abilities	96
	The value and limitations of mental tests	98
	Further reading	101
	Bibliography	105

Preface

The emergence of modern educational psychology as a separate discipline with its own distinctive aims and methods has taken place against a rich background of prior knowledge about children's learning and development. The aim of the present volume is to outline the more important of these ideas and experiments and to show how, in their various ways, they have all helped to shape our present understanding of the factors that influence child life and growth.

For convenience, each of the major divisions of educational psychology—the study of learning, child development and the psychology of individual differences—is treated separately and consists of an account of the concepts and movements which, over the past two hundred years or so, have contributed to a better understanding of children's behaviour and progress.

Many contemporary issues in educational psychology become clearer when set against the perspective of their historical antecedents. Within such a context, fresh assessments of problems both classical and current may be made —partly through a study of the work of the great writers and experimenters in the history of psychology and partly by means of recent informed opinion on their views.

Valuable material for the present book was obtained

PREFACE

from several sources, namely Gardner Murphy's *Historical Introduction to Modern Psychology*, R. S. Peter's revision of *Brett's History of Psychology*, Quick's *Essays on Educational Reformers*, Garrett's *Great Experiments in Psychology*, and Mandler's and Kessen's *Perspectives in Psychology*. Without the erudite commentaries and happy diversities these books contain, the present work would not have been possible.

E. G. S. EVANS

1
Child development

Introduction

A remarkable fact of the present century is the unprecedented interest in the study of children—in the development of their natural life processes and abilities, in the effects of early upbringing on their adjustment to home and school and in the influence of unconscious motivations and conflicts on their thinking and general behaviour. But child psychology was not unknown in previous times, especially in the eighteenth and nineteenth centuries. This is clearly evident in the writings of the precursors of the child study movement—Rousseau, Pestalozzi, and Froebel —all of whom drew attention to the different stages through which children pass in their development and emphasized the need to educate them through their own self-activity and natural capacities.

Closely following the work of these early educationists came the influence of the theory of evolution which, from the mid-nineteenth century onwards, awakened an even greater interest in the study of children. In considering the effect evolutionary doctrine had on the development of child psychology, the writings of three Englishmen—

CHILD DEVELOPMENT

Spencer, Darwin and Galton—were outstanding, and their investigations were quickly followed by other more systematic studies of children. These were of three main kinds: (a) studies of the child mind, as seen in the investigations of Preyer, Sully, Isaacs and Piaget; (b) behavioural studies, mainly American, and associated with the work of Watson, Hall and Gesell; (c) studies of childhood conflicts, stemming from the enquiries of Freud, Anna Freud, Melanie Klein and their co-workers.

Precursors

Jean-Jacques Rousseau (1712-1778). If a date is needed to mark the beginning of child psychology it is 1762 when Rousseau published the *Émile, or On Education*. In this book Rousseau distinguished the various stages of child development which Rusk (1954) has summarized as follows: (i) infancy characterized by habit and the training of the emotions; (ii) childhood characterized by 'necessity' and the training of the senses; (iii) boyhood characterized by 'utility' and the training of the intellect; (iv) adolescence, the stage of 'morality' and of moral aesthetic and social education.

Some fifty years ago the Swiss educational psychologist, Claparede, speaking on the bicentennial of Rousseau's birth, ascribed to the *Émile* certain fundamental principles of child behaviour which Kessen (1965) refers to as follows:

The Law of Genetic Succession: The child develops naturally by passing through a number of stages that succeed one another in a constant order.
The Law of Genetico-Functional Exercise: This law really implies two, which can be stated in the following

way. (a) The exercise of a function is necessary to its development . . . (b) The exercise of a function is necessary to the appearance of certain other functions. . . .
The Law of Functional Adaptation: That action will be elicited which serves to satisfy the need or the interest of the moment. . . .
The Law of Functional Autonomy: The child is not, considered in himself, an imperfect being; he is a being adapted to circumstances which are appropriate for him; his mental activity is appropriate to his needs, and his mental life is integrated. . . .
The Law of Individuality: Every person differs more or less, in physical and psychological characteristics, from other people. . . .

These somewhat formal statements represent the most important of Rousseau's ideas about children's mental development. The first, that of genetic succession, shows that Rousseau recognized that nature had endowed the child with certain stages of development to ensure his healthy growth. The order of development started from simple sensory experiences and these were followed in turn by the appearance of higher mental processes—images, perceptions, ideas, reason and judgment. Of all these, however, none was as important to Rousseau as the child's emotional development. The following quotations from the *Émile* illustrate this clearly.

> The child's first mental experiences are purely affective, he is only aware of pleasure and pain; it takes him a long time to acquire the definite sensations which show him things outside himself, but before these things present and withdraw themselves, so to speak, from his sight, taking size and shape for him, the recurrence of evolutional experiences is beginning to subject the child to the rule of habit.

CHILD DEVELOPMENT

Even more significant for the child's subsequent development are the changes in temperament and character that occur at adolescence.

> As the roaring of the waves precedes the tempest, so the murmur of rising passions announces this tumultuous change, a suppressed excitement warns us of the approaching danger. A change of temper, frequent outbreaks of anger, a perpetual stirring of the mind, make the child almost ungovernable. He becomes deaf to the voice he used to obey; he is a lion in a fever; he distrusts his keeper and refuses to be controlled.
>
> With the moral symptoms of a changing temper there are perceptible changes in appearance. His countenance develops and takes the stamp of his character, the soft and sparse down upon his cheeks becomes darker and stiffer. His voice grows hoarse or rather he loses it altogether. He is neither a child nor a man and cannot speak like either of them. His eyes, those organs of the soul which till now were dumb, find speech and meaning; a kindling fire illumines them, there is still a sacred innocence in their brightening glance, but they have lost their first meaningless expression; he is already aware that they can say too much; he is beginning to learn to lower his eyes and blush, he is becoming sensitive, though he does not know what it is that he feels; he is uneasy without knowing why. All this may happen gradually and give you time enough; but if his keenness becomes impatience, his eagerness, madness, if he is angry and sorry, all in a moment, if he weeps without cause, if in the presence of objects which are beginning to be a source of danger, his pulse quickens and his eyes sparkle, if he trembles when a woman's hand touches his, if he is troubled or timid in her presence, O Ulysses, wise Ulysses! have a care! The passages you closed with so much pain are open; the winds are un-

loosed; keep your hand upon the helm or all is lost (Kessen).

Several educational implications stem from an acceptance of Rousseau's views.

Childhood is natural and exists in its own right. As Kessen has written:

> Childhood is not a time set aside for adults to finish God's work, to bring the child (whether filled with sin or epistemologically and morally empty) steadily into closer match with adult behaviour. Childhood is a time important in itself, a time when the behaviour of the child is appropriate to the demands of his needs and his world. Whenever one looks at a child, newborn, in school, adolescent, one sees a whole human being, properly put together for his particular time. It is as well to consider the ape to be an incomplete man as to consider the child to be an incomplete adult. Moreover, Rousseau pointed out that the teacher and parent had better consider the integrity of the child; the educator who proceeded blind to the nature (the naturalness, the integrity) of childhood would produce an ill-made human being.

The acceptance by teachers of the priority of natural development, or as Kessen again points out: '. . . of the normal succession of stages in growth, and especially of the coherence of the child's mind at every stage—and tailor his pedagogy to the child'.

Above all, Rousseau firmly believed that the child should be permitted to grow up without much adult supervision and direction.

> Oh, wise man, take time to observe nature; watch your scholar well before you say a word to him; first leave the germ of his character free to show itself, do not

constrain him in anything, the better to see him as he really is. . . .

Zealous teachers, be simple, sensible and reticent; be in no hurry to act unless to prevent the actions of others. Again and again I say, reject, if it may be, a good lesson for fear of giving a bad one. Beware of playing the tempter in this world, which nature intended as an earthly paradise for men, and do not attempt to give the innocent child the knowledge of good and evil; since you cannot prevent the child learning by what he sees outside himself, restrict your own efforts to impressing those examples on his mind in the form best suited for him!

The relation of the child to the world is an active searching one. Kessen has expressed Rousseau's attitude as follows:

The child engages his environment, using it to suit his interests. He fits his abilities to the world in play and in the solving of problems, not as a passive recipient of the tutor's instruction, nor as a victim of Hume's contingencies, but as a busy, testing, motivated explorer. Knowledge is not an invention of adults poured into willing or unwilling vessels; it is a joint construction of the child in nature and the natural world.

Rousseau's enduring contribution to education, therefore, was his insistence on the importance of the natural stages of mental development in childhood and adolescence, especially emotional development, which he tended to emphasize to the neglect of the individual's social development.

Johann Heinrich Pestalozzi (1746-1827) Another precursor of modern child psychology, moved by Rousseau's vision, was Johann Heinrich Pestalozzi (1746-1827). He, more than Rousseau, recognized the importance of all aspects of a child's development, and in his writings expressed a point of view which was committed to the need for parents and teachers alike to give, before all else, loving care, sympathy and attention to children, especially in their early education. For Pestalozzi, the child's mother was the first and most important educator. This fact, and his emphasis that learning must be based on the activity of the child, are the essential features of the Pestalozzi method.

Pestalozzi built his theory of children round the notion of *Anschauung*, a difficult word to define in English. It denotes an active principle of mind and, more specifically, the means by which a child comes to acquire some sort of personal faith, identity, and integrity for himself and, at the same time, an appreciation of the world around him—a world-picture and a vision of life. *Anschauung* bears slight relation to Spearman's (1923) principles of cognition and neogenesis, being much more comprehensive than these. It is closer to Herbart's (1816) concept of apperception, which came from Leibnitz and refers to the totality of conscious activities that are involved in the choice of interpretation of anything, i.e. the sum total of all experiences that are involved in giving meaning to anything. Again, *Anschauung* has affiliation with Burt's (1955) view of intelligence as the 'integrative capacity of mind' and with Piaget's (1947) notion that a child's mental life is essentially active and constructive and intimately bound up with language, play and the whole physical and social world.

But Pestalozzi also believed that *Anschauung* would not develop naturally by itself and, moreover, could be weakened and destroyed by the educational practices of his day. He therefore proceeded to devise his own educational programme consisting of exercises, drills and techniques which aimed to develop *Anschauung* to the fullest possible extent. Pestalozzi claimed that by starting from children's early sense impressions and from what they observe for themselves, three fundamental elements of knowledge—language, form and number—could be built up and thus used to foster *Anschauung*.

Pestalozzi expresses this as follows:

> Friend! When I now look back and ask myself: What have I especially done for the very being of education? I find I have fixed the highest, supreme principle of instruction in the recognition of sense-impression as the absolute foundation of all knowledge. Apart from all special teaching I have sought to discover the nature of teaching itself; and the prototype, by which Nature herself has determined the instruction to three elementary means (form, number and language); and have sought for special methods which should render the results of all instruction in these three branches absolutely certain.
>
> Lastly, I have brought these three elementary means into harmony with each other, and made instruction, in all three branches, not only harmonious with itself in many ways, but also with human nature and have brought it nearer to the course of Nature in the development of the human race (Kessen).

By the same means, the child's own personal integrity and individuality were able to be secured so that he becomes somebody unique and complete in himself. For Pestalozzi, 'being' somebody is far more important than acquiring knowledge. He states: 'The reading, writing and arithmetic are not after all what they most need. It is well and good for them to learn something, but the really important thing for them is to *be* something' (Quick, 1895). For Pestalozzi, 'being' was as important as 'doing'. Again and again he maintains that 'being' and 'doing' come before 'knowing', that knowledge is utterly valueless unless it is based on action. In *Leonard and Gertrude* he writes:

> Although Gertrude exerted herself to develop very early the manual dexterity of her children, she was in no haste for them to learn to read and write; but she took pains to teach them early how to speak; for, as she said, 'Of what use is it for a person to be able to read and write if he cannot speak, since reading and writing are only an artificial sort of speech'. . . . She did not adopt the tone of an instructor towards the children . . . and her verbal instruction seemed to vanish in the spirit of her real activity, in which it always had its source. The result of her system was that each child was skilful, intelligent and active to the full extent that its age and development allowed (Quick).

Although Pestalozzi believed that learning must be based on the activity of the child, developed through *Anschauung*, it could not be achieved without the background of a loving home and mother. The importance Pestalozzi attaches to this is evident in the following quotations from *How Gertrude Teaches her Children*.

> From the moment that a mother takes a child upon her lap, she teaches him. She brings nearer to his senses what nature has scattered afar off over large areas and in confusion, and makes the action of receiving sense-impressions and the knowledge derived from them, easy, pleasant and delightful to him.
> The mother, weak and untrained follows Nature, without help or guidance, and knows not what she is doing.

CHILD DEVELOPMENT

> She does not intend to teach, she intends only to quiet the child, to occupy him. But, nevertheless, in her pure simplicity she follows the high course of Nature without knowing what Nature does through her; and Nature does very much through her. In this way she opens the world to the child. She makes him ready to use his senses, and prepares for the early development of his attention and power of observation (Kessen).

The same attitude is expressed in a paper called the *Swiss Journal* which Pestalozzi started in 1782.

> The child at his mother's breast is weaker and more dependent than any other creature on earth, and yet he already feels the first moral impression of love and gratitude. Morality is nothing but a result of the development of the first sentiments of love and gratitude felt by the infant (Quick).

The great earnestness with which Pestalozzi addressed himself to mothers was prompted by a belief that the powers they possessed over their infants was of a God-given quality.

> The mother is qualified, and qualified by the Creator Himself to become the principal agent in the development of her child . . . and what is demanded of her is—*a thinking love.* . . . God has given to thy child all the faculties of our nature, but the grand point remains undecided—how shall this heart, this head, these hands, be employed? To whose service shall they be dedicated? (Quick).
>
> Maternal love is the first agent in education. . . . Through it the child is led to love and trust his Creator and his Redeemer (Quick).

The attitudes expressed in these quotations, along with

the loving care and devotion that Pestalozzi himself gave to the deprived and neglected pupils in his schools at Neuhof, Stanz, Burgdorf and Yverdun, reflect, as nothing else does, his essential Christian humanity.

In an article Pestalozzi wrote in a paper called *Ephemerides* in 1775, he says of these children:

> I have proved that it is not regular work that stops the development of so many poor children, but the turmoil and irregularity of their lives, the privations they endure, the excesses they indulge in when opportunity offers, the wild rebellious passions so seldom restrained, and the hopelessness to which they are so often a prey. I have proved that children, after having lost health, strength and courage in a life of idleness and mendacity have, when once set to regular work, quickly recovered their health and spirits and grown rapidly. I have found that when taken out of their abject condition they soon become kindly, trustful and sympathetic; that even the more degraded of them are touched by kindness, and that the eyes of the child who has been steeped in misery, grow bright with pleasure and surprise, when after years of hardship he sees a gentle friendly hand stretched out to help him; and I am convinced that *when a child's heart has been troubled the consequences will be great for his development and entire moral character* (Quick).

In summarizing Pestalozzi's contributions to education and psychology, we may say that he not only recognized that teaching must be based on the natural stages of a child's development but realized that a sound knowledge of the basic skills was essential to this development and to the individual's subsequent progress in school. More than any other man Pestalozzi put teaching on a psychological basis, believing in so doing, however, that the true function

CHILD DEVELOPMENT

of education was not merely to teach but to develop the child through love. 'The essential principle of education is not teaching,' said Pestalozzi, 'it is love. . . . The child loves and believes before it thinks and acts' (Quick). Putting it another way, the simple but great truth that Pestalozzi had hit upon was that a teacher must have a heart, for only in this way can his soul kindle another's. The greatest educating force is thus the teacher's personality. Nothing can touch it or replace it and in no other way, as our dreamer of dreams so clearly saw, could a child attain to the true dignity and responsibilities of man.

Friedrich Froebel (1783-1852) Froebel's great work, *The Education of Man*, was first published in 1826 and his first kindergarten or 'Garden of Children', opened in the village of Blankenberg in 1837. The school had to be abandoned for lack of funds, so Froebel carried on courses for young teachers, first at Keilhan, and from 1848 until his death in 1852, at Lieberheim and in the duchy of Meiningen.

Through his writings and teaching Froebel became firmly established as a great visionary whose ideas of educating young children in accordance with their self-activity and natural stages of growth had a profound effect upon both the aims and methods of child education in Germany.

The last four years of his life were his happiest and most peaceful but in 1851 an edict was issued forbidding the establishment of his schools in Germany. This was brought about through an erroneous association, in the mind of the cultus-minister Raumer, of Froebel's work with the socialist writings of a nephew, Karl Froebel. In spite of protests from a congress of schoolmasters against the calumnious decree, it remained in force and Froebel

CHILD DEVELOPMENT

did not survive long afterwards. But his ideas lived on amongst his students and followers and have since made him yet another of the great precursors of modern educational practice.

Froebel strove passionately all his life to arrive, through logical-speculative methods, at a true conception of child development. According to Quick: 'More and more the thought possessed him that the one thing needful for man was unity of development, perfect evolution in accordance with the laws of his being, evolution as science discovers in the other organisms of nature.'

Froebel's ideas were based on the belief that children's behaviour and experiences become increasingly more complex and specialized through their own spontaneous self-activity, which he saw as the one true starting point in their development and which, in itself, was based on a divine principle. He regarded self-activity as a 'formative and creative instinct' and regarded it as the real basis of all learning—that children learn through it and, by this means and this means alone, become both doers and creators.

Great prominence was given by Froebel, not only to the early years of childhood, but to all the succeeding stages of development. He maintained that each of these had a distinctiveness and completeness of its own which could only be achieved through perfection of the earlier stage. He emphasized particularly children's restlessness of body and mind, their fondness for using their hands, their curiosity and sociability, as well as their moral and sympathetic natures. But these needed to be cultivated and controlled in their education and the way this was to be achieved was through play. Froebel saw play as a distinctly educational objective which, in his own words, was 'to give the children employment in agreement with their whole nature, to strengthen their bodies, to exercise their senses, to engage their awakening mind, and through their senses, to bring them acquainted with nature and their fellow-creatures; it is especially to guide the heart and the affections and to lead them to the original ground of all life, to unity with themselves'.

As all education was to be sought in play, Froebel devised a series of activities and materials which aimed to develop the children's inventiveness and creativity. Particular attention was given to the training of the senses, especially those of sight, sound, touch, rhythm and motion. Intuition was also encouraged but the mechanical and formal learning of facts, so prominent in German schools, was to be rigorously excluded. All the time, the emphasis was placed on the children's mental activity and dynamic growth and on their need to see meaning and purpose in their activities at all stages of their development.

The influence of Evolutionism

The main driving force which, from the mid-nineteenth century onwards focused attention on the study of children, came from the theory of evolution. Evolutionism postulated levels of development of the mind, and, as Rousseau, Pestalozzi and Froebel had previously asserted, it emphasized the need to let the child develop his natural abilities and interests.

Charles Darwin (1809-1882) The doctrine was outlined in Darwin's *Origin of Species* which first appeared in 1859 and, as Peters (1962) has pointed out, 'stimulated interest

CHILD DEVELOPMENT

in the development of the child as a field of biological study'. The same viewpoint appeared even earlier in Spencer's *Developmental Hypothesis* of 1852 and in his *Principles of Psychology* of 1855.

Herbert Spencer (1820-1903) Spencer's writings on both education and psychology drew attention to children as children, that they existed as individuals in their own right and that their growth and learning reflected the vital processes of heredity, continuous variation and adaptation upon which life itself was founded.

Corresponding to life, too, Spencer's hypothesis laid down levels of mental development which kept pace with the development of the central nervous system in the individual and ranged from the simplest reflexes and associations to such complex and highly integrated functions as memory, perception and reason. Writing in 1896, Spencer described the processes as follows:

> The development of the mind, as all other development, is an advance from the indefinite to the definite. In common with the rest of the organism the brain reaches its finished structure only at maturity; and in proportion as structure is unfinished, its actions are wanting in precision. Hence like the first movements and the first attempts at speech, the first perceptions and thoughts are extremely vague. As from a rudimentary eye, discerning only the difference between light and darkness, the progress is to an eye that distinguishes kinds and graduations of colour, and details of form, with the greatest exactness; so, the intellect as a whole and in each faculty, beginning with the modest discriminations among objects and actions, advances towards discriminations of increasing nicety and distinctness. To

this general law our educational course and methods must conform (p. 66 *Education: Intellectual, Moral and Physical*, 1896).

Spencer also maintained that the gradual emergence of mental abilities in the individual reproduced in abbreviated form the evolution of the human race, and that children's education should be shaped to accord with this supposed truth. This view, known as the Recapitulation Theory, attempted to deduce the course of psychological development from the facts of embryological growth, on the one hand, and, on the other, from a theory that had been proposed some years earlier by the French biologist Lamarck (1744-1829). Lamarck claimed that adaptive variations brought about by the environment could be inherited. As a consequence of this view, 'The individual child is assumed to inherit the capacities, memories, and habits of a long line of ancestors, pre-historic and civilized, and to exhibit them stage by stage in much the same order as that in which they were originally acquired' (Hadow Report, H.M.S.O., 1931).

The plausible generalizations of the Recapitulation Theory are, of course, no longer accepted, especially insofar as they relate to the biological transmission of acquired psychological characteristics. Children, in their mental development, do not climb up their own genealogical tree. Their interests and behaviour are not inherited and, like other psychological traits, cannot be deduced from the fundamental assumptions of Recapitulation Theory. As Burt has pointed out: 'Such deductions may prompt suggestive hypotheses for research or generalization, but the distinctive features at each stage must be discovered by a direct application of experimental tests, or of controlled statistical observation, to the study of psychological qualities at first hand' (Hadow Report, H.M.S.O., 1931).

In summarizing the effects of Evolutionism on the study of children from the mid-nineteenth century to its close, we may say that its approach was predominantly biological and anthropological. As Rousseau, Pestalozzi and Froebel had done beforehand, it encouraged a more imaginative approach to children's upbringing that was in accordance with their actual interests and capacities. It also stressed the common aspects of development in both the race and the individual but, in so doing, tended to over-emphasize the maturational processes of development to the exclusion of social and cultural factors.

Many studies at this time were also unsystematic and inclined to introspection and it was not until the beginning of the present century that a more scientific and objective approach was adopted towards children's development.

Systematic studies of children

The beginnings of systematic child psychology are usually ascribed to the German psychologist, W. T. Preyer, who in *The Mind of the Child* (1881) described, from direct observations, his studies of imitation, instincts and other expressive functions in young children with, as Flugel (1953) has put it, 'the gradual complications ensuing as a result of experience and learning'. Like earlier studies, however, Preyer's work was much criticized because of its inadequate separation of observation from introspection.

Another investigator was the American, Stanley Hall, who in 1891 founded *Pedagogical Seminary*, a journal devoted to child study. Hall embarked on studies of the ideas, attitudes, and personalities of children and this culminated in his monumental work entitled *Adolescence* (1904). Shortly after the appearance of *Pedagogical Seminary*, Witmer established in 1897, in Philadelphia, a psychological clinic for the study of maladjustment in children, the forerunner of the modern child guidance clinic. Some time later, in Germany, Stern embarked on his systematic investigations of individual differences in children's perceptions, recall and other cognitive processes which he regarded as expressions of differences in temperament and attitude.

James Sully (1842-1923) These early studies of the child mind both in Germany and America were accompanied in Britain by the work of James Sully, the first notable worker in the field of child development in this country. Sully made many careful observations of different aspects of child behaviour—their language, play, laughter, thought processes, imagination and so on. He also founded The British Association for Child Study (1893) which, like Hall's *Pedagogical Seminary* played an important part in the development of the 'new education movement'.

Susan Isaacs (1885-1948) After Sully came Susan Isaacs whose studies of the social and intellectual processes of young children and their spontaneous behaviour in the free atmosphere of the Malting House School, Cambridge, had a tremendous impact upon teaching aims and methods in the period 1930-40.

One of Isaacs's most important researches was concerned with the children's intelligence, in which she showed how their thinking processes work in the actual pursuit of their practical and theoretical interests. She classified the pupil's responses into the following categories:

The application of knowledge already possessed to new situations and problems, as when Tommy and Christopher had a conversation about steam and Christopher said, 'Steam's really water but it's not the same as the steam of the bonfire.'

Increase of knowledge. A second type of behaviour was related to the direct increase of knowledge, in contrast to the application of what the children already knew. An example of this occurred when one pupil brought in a glass jar full of snow and put it on the radiator to melt. The children kept looking at it and when it was melted said, 'What a little bit of water it has made.'

Social interchange of knowledge. This included children's 'why' questions and 'becauses' and other logical queries and reasoning, as well as social discussions with corrections and self-corrections. Isaacs regarded children's 'why' questions as presenting a specific problem, obstruction or contradiction to be resolved by the child—a view that was somewhat different from that held by Piaget. Piaget regarded the 'why' as a mere stimulus action which set the machinery of the child's thoughts in motion, the nature of the motion then being a function of the machinery which, in his view, was (as we shall shortly see) the egocentric structure of the child's mind.

Isaac's book *Intellectual Growth in Young Children* (1930) was followed by *The Children we Teach* (1932), and *Social Development in Young Children* (1933). All this work was marked by careful observation and the detailed collection of masses of incidents relating to the behaviour of children aged 3-11 years; as such it represents the most significant contribution made by a British child psychologist during the third and fourth decades of the century.

Arnold Gesell (1880-1961) Arnold Gesell continued, in America, the tradition laid down by Darwin and Galton. He refused to be moved by the findings of psychoanalysis and the new experimental studies of learning and conditioning, remaining to the last a staunch hereditarian. He established a clinic for child study and research at Yale where his work, both clinical and theoretical, was concerned mainly with infants and young children.

Gesell regarded maturation as the central concept in child psychology and the necessary condition of developmental change. He writes:

> The supreme genetic law appears to be this: All present growth hinges on part growth. Growth is not a simple function neatly determined by X units of inheritance plus Y units of environment, but is an historical concept which reflects at every stage the part which it incorporates.

Again, Gesell states:

> All things considered, the inevitableness and surety of maturation are the most impressive characteristics of early development. It is the hereditary ballast which conserves and stabilizes the growth of each individual infant. It is indigenous in its compulsion; but we may well be grateful for this degree of determiness. If it did not exist the infant would be a victim of a flaccid maleability which is sometimes romantically ascribed to him. His mind, his spirit, his personality would fall a ready prey to disease, to starvation, to malnutrition, and worst of all to misguided management. As it is, the inborn tendency toward optimum development is so

CHILD DEVELOPMENT

inveterate that he benefits liberally from what is good in our practice and suffers less than he logically should from our unenlightenment.

Gesell built up a large body of observations on the development of young children's behaviour, attributing by far the greater part of it to genetic influences. Thus, of 'handedness', he says: 'social conditioning cannot overcome left handedness'; and the same belief is expressed about the inheritance of other specific abilities. 'Specific ability in drawing, special interest in music, marked sociability, early facility in language, precocity in the use of generalizations and abstractions, all these manifest themselves in infancy in a way suggestive of native gifts or predispositions. If conditioning during infancy were responsible for such individual differences, there would be much more similarity between siblings and twins than is actually found.'

A similar view is expressed concerning a child's temperamental characteristics. 'It is doubtful whether the basic temperamental qualities of infants can be measureably altered by environmental influences. Training and hygiene may exert very palpable and important influences in the organization of the personality without necessarily altering the underlying natural or habitus.'

Thus, when considering the early genesis of individual differences in children, whether it be specific abilities and aptitudes or differences in temperament, Gesell's researches let him believe that the constitutional qualities of the child far outweighed environmental influences. The contribution of the latter he held to be relatively slight for though, in his words, 'environmental factors support, inflict and modify, they do not generate the progressions of development.'

An important exception, recognized by Gesell, was to be found in the formation of personality when he wrote: 'Growth potency is fundamentally dependent on original equipment; but the personality make-up is almost literally fabricated by the social conditions in which the young mind grows.' And again, he states: '. . . the personality configuration of the child is not determined by germinal constitution . . . it is a product of growth regulation. The regulation is accompanied, both consciously and unconsciously, through the sound interaction between the young child and his household. The association of parent and child is a kind of psychological partnership.'

As an articulate spokesman for maturation, Gesell's influence was far-reaching and from the mid-1920s his descriptive works received avid receptions, especially from mothers and other people concerned with the upbringing of young children. His principal books were *Infancy and Human Growth* (1928), *An Atlas of Infant Behaviour* (1934), *Developmental Diagnosis* (1940) and *Infant and Child in the Culture of Today* (1943).

Since Gesell dealt mainly with infants and pre-school children his researches have not attracted the same degree of interest that frequently attaches to writers of the later stages of childhood. His work, nevertheless, has always been of great interest and significance to educationalists; and in bringing together a mass of evidence bearing on the claims of heredity his convictions seem, in many ways, to be less extravagant than those of another American, the behaviourist, J. B. Watson, who presented a sharply contrasted doctrine of child development.

John Brodus Watson (1878-1958) Between 1913 and 1920 Watson invented a new kind of psychology called

CHILD DEVELOPMENT

Behaviourism. It emphasized that the contribution of environmental experiences and learning to the development of children is infinitely more important than the mark of heredity. At the same time, Behaviourism was a violent reaction against the introspective analysis and description of conscious experience which, at the beginning of the twentieth century, characterized experimental psychology in Germany and America.

Watson's premise was that psychology, from first to last, should be an objective branch of natural science and should have, as its aim, the prediction and control of human behaviour. Its methods should involve no introspection and no interpretation of its data in terms of consciousness or mind. For Watson, these were meaningless concepts.

Helped by the discovery by Pavlov, in 1915, of the conditioned response, Watson shortly afterwards began his own systematic observations of children. He investigated the reflex equipment of new-born infants, outlined a theory of emotional development based on the three unconditioned reflexes of fear, rage, and love and demonstrated experimentally how the learning and extinction of fears in a child could occur through the process of conditioning.

One of Watson's most significant contributions was his proposal that parents could train their children to be anything they wished. He writes:

> Children's fears are home-grown just like their loves and temper outbursts. The parents do the emotional planning and the cultivating. At three years of age the child's whole emotional life plan has been laid down, his emotional disposition set. At that age the parents have already determined for him whether he is to

grow into a happy person, wholesome and good-natured, whether he is to be a whining complaining neurotic, an anger-driven, vindictive, over-bearing slave driver, or one whose every move in life is definitely controlled by fear.

Children's fears, for Watson, could be easily learned and controlled through conditioning and he regarded some fear-training in the home as necessary. He says:

To get the right psychological conditions, the parents should always apply this painful stimulus just at the moment the undesirable act is taking place. If you wait for father to spank when he gets home it is practically impossible to establish a conditioned negative response. Unless negatively conditioned in this way how else will children learn not to reach for glasses and vases? How can they learn not to touch strange dogs, fondle strange cats, to walk out into the water? . . . We can sum it all up by saying that the behaviourist advocates the early building in of appropriate commonsense negative reactions by the method of gently rapping the fingers or hand or other bodily part when the undesirable act is taking place, but as an objective experimental procedure—never as punishment.

Watson was also aware of the dangers of too much mother-love and coddling in the upbringing of young children. He looked upon this as an unnecessary form of over-conditioning, as a hindrance to development. He wrote:

There is a sensible way of treating children. Treat them as though they were young adults. Dress them, bathe them with care and circumspection. Let your behaviour always be objective and kindly-firm. Never hug or kiss them, never let them sit on your lap. If you must, kiss them once on the forehead when they say good night. Shake hands with them in the morning. Give them a pat on the head if they have made an extraordinarily good job of a difficult task. Try it out. In a week's time you will find how easy it is to be perfectly objective with your child and at the same time kindly. You will be utterly ashamed of the mawkish sentimental way you have been handling it.

Watson's writings changed the whole tone of child psychology in America and exerted a strong influence on child rearing procedures for several decades. His beliefs became models for researches into the behaviour of children and although his methods were too narrow to embrace the wide variety of children's thinking and emotions, he brought about a revolution in psychology, did much to free it from subjectivism and make it a scientific topic of study.

Jean Piaget (1896-) An even more significant writer whose early studies we must now discuss is Jean Piaget. His researches began to be published in English in 1924 and since that time he has conducted numerous enquiries into children's intellectual development and thought processes. It is not possible to consider all of his major works here and our summary will be restricted to a description of three of them, *Language and Thought of the Child* (1924), *The Child's Conception of Physical Causality* (1927) and *The Psychology of Intelligence* (1947).

In *Language and Thought of the Child*, Piaget was chiefly interested in the way in which children's language expresses their thoughts. He recognized two major types of speech (a) *egocentric speech*, and (b) *socialized speech*.

Egocentric speech consisted of echolalia, the monologue,

and the dual or collective monologue, and was said to occur prominently in the early years up to the ages of 3-5. During this period 'the child does not bother to know to whom he is speaking nor whether he is being listened to. He talks either to himself or for the pleasure of associating anyone who happens to be there with the activity of the moment.' In other words, he does not attempt to place himself at the point of view of his hearer.

The second type of speech, socialized speech, occurs, according to Piaget, with increasing frequency at 7-8 years. Piaget means by socialized speech, speech 'in which the child addresses his hearer, considers his point of view, tries to influence him or actually exchanges ideas with him.' Such speech consists of those situations when 'the child really exchanges his thoughts with others; it also consists of criticism, commands, threats, questions and answers'.

A number of investigators have since tended to place the appearance of socialized speech a lot earlier than Piaget, claiming that at least 80 per cent of the speech of pre-school children is definitely socialized and that with primary infants the percentage is even higher. Indeed, it is said that the flow of speech which often accompanies a young child's activity is really an expression of a need for social contact and that when they talk they usually do so about things which have not only a sound contact for them but an emotional one as well. A further criticism is given by Isaacs who believed that the social interests of the child are not, as Piaget implies, a simple and direct expression of a biological process of maturation. Isaacs claimed instead that socialization possesses a strictly psychological genesis and that the form of socialization is the outcome of a highly complicated interplay of tendencies and counter-tendencies. There is no doubt that Piaget would agree with this and, in his later work, the influence of social factors on intellectual development is made perfectly clear.

Another of Piaget's earlier researches was *The Child's Conception of Physical Causality* which examines the child's ideas about natural phenomena like wind, air, natural movement and physical force. As a result of his experiments Piaget concluded that no genuine physical explanation of natural phenomena can be given by children much before the ages of 7-8 years. From 5 years up to 7-8 years most of the reasons or explanations put forward by children are mystical, magical, animistic or dynamic. They cannot explain simple, natural happenings on rational, logical or mechanical grounds. For the young child the whole of life is teeming with subjective and psychological elements and, from their point of view, natural happenings cannot be explained in any other way. Rational types of explanation are quite beyond them.

After 7-8 years, however, more positive forms of explanation gradually supplant the others and by about 11-12 years the evolution is complete.

The reason given by Piaget for the period of precausality in children is that there is, in the child's mind, a confusion of the self and the universe; a gradual separation and objectification then occurs which goes hand in hand with the development of the self or ego, and this results in more logical forms of explanation being used by the child in his explanation of the phenomena.

Some ten years after the publication of *The Child's Conception of Physical Causality* appeared *The Origin of Intelligence in Young Children* (1936) and this was followed in 1947 by one of the most important of Piaget's studies, namely, *The Psychology of Intelligence*. In it are outlined the stages of thought a child passes through from birth to adolescence. They are as follows:

The period of sensori-motor intelligence, which extends from birth up to about eighteen months. It is characterized firstly, by the appearance of simple sensory and motor activities and later by the development of simple habits and associations.

The symbolic, pre-conceptual period, from eighteen months up to nearly four years, is marked by the appearance of language, by imitating words and attaching vague meanings to them. There also appears symbolic play, deferred imitation and what Piaget calls 'pre-concepts', i.e. ideas which the child attaches to the verbal signs he uses—ideas which lie mid-way between the generality of real concepts and the individuality of the elements composing them.

The period of intuitive and representative thought, from 4 to 7-8 years, is characterized firstly by the illogical, inconsistent and egocentric nature of the child's thinking at this time, and secondly by the fact that many of his ideas and images are now detached from reality and become represented in imitation and in play and through language and social intercourse.

The period of concrete operations, from 7-8 to 11-12 years, consists of genuine internal operations or actions which are grouped and organized around objects or things that can be manipulated or known through the senses. The child's intelligence is now much more logical and consistent, much more systematic and deductive but tied, in the main, to practical, concrete situations and not yet detached from their contents.

The period of formal thought, from 11-12 years to adolescence shows that the child possesses still greater powers of deduction and abstraction and this leads gradually to reflective thinking of the adult kind, consisting of operations, of judgment and other forms of reasoning and formal relation-finding.

According to Piaget, these stages in the child's thought represent a functional continuity, each phase springing from a previous one and all building up to form a hierarchy of mental operation which depends, for its appearance, both on innate, maturational factors and on social and cultural influences.

The other essential feature of Piaget's psychology is that intelligence in the child is something essentially active and constructive. For Piaget, the child's mind cannot remain passive in the face of ideas; in order to understand these ideas the child must reconstruct them for himself. He does this through the development of 'operations', i.e. genuine, internal mental actions such as being able to combine and associate things in different ways, to reverse and conserve things.

In more general terms, we may say that Piaget believed the human mind to be essentially historical and that intelligence begins only when past experiences influence present behaviour. Piaget's view starts from the biological concept of *adaptation* which he sees as an interplay of two complementary processes, *assimilation* and *accommodation*. Assimilation occurs whenever a child uses something in his environment for some activity which is already part of his repertoire, whenever something new is understood in terms of something already familiar. Accommodation, on the other hand, means the acquisition of new activities to a child's behaviour or a change in old activities in response to environmental events. Berlyne (1957) has said:

> ... assimilation seems to include what learning theories call generalization and discrimination processes, determining which particular response a particular stimulus will elicit, while accommodation covers 'differentiation of responses' and the learning of new responses.

Piaget's studies of children's intelligence have not, of course, escaped criticism, especially the way he ignores emotional and motivational factors, the inadequacy of his sampling procedures, his lack of statistical controls and what Pratt describes as 'his subjective approach to the analysis of child behaviour' which the same critic says is 'little removed from ordinary literary speculation'.

On the positive side, however, Piaget's experiments are repeatable and many British investigators have demonstrated the validity of his findings, e.g. that the succession of intellectual changes in the child seem to be constant even though the age at which they appear tends to be relative to the environment. From an educational point of view also, Piaget's work has many important implications. Thus, his stages or sequence of changes relate very closely to modern views concerning readiness for learning certain educational skills. Again, the results of many of his experiments point to the futility of teaching mechanical formulae when a child is not ready to understand the operations involved. His work emphasizes how important it is to proceed from the concrete to the abstract in teaching and that many formal methods should be used only when the child's perceptions and intuitions have become systematized. Finally, Piaget's investigations have shown how different the child's ideas about the world are from our own. The young child up to seven or eight years, for example, thinks very largely in terms of his intuitions. From 7-8 years up to 11 or 12 he thinks not in formal terms but in the concrete and in terms of his perceptions and this continues until the level of formal hypothetical deductive operations is reached.

Piaget's studies have in this way provided the means for a better understanding of children's learning and although, as Kessen (1965) points out, the portrait of the child's intelligence that is depicted is 'incomplete, provocative and of uncertain promise', it presents a far more comprehensive picture of the child's mind than was known before. The insight that Piaget has shown into the nature of the learning process is of particular significance; but this most intractable of processes—the psychology of learning—will be discussed in a later chapter.

Summary

The earliest studies of children's development which occurred towards the close of the nineteenth century exhibited a biological orientation and were limited to simple, straightforward observations and descriptions of children's behaviour. Evolutionary theory was the revolutionary influence at this time and postulated levels of development of the mind and as a result, both British and European investigators concerned themselves with the development of the child's natural abilities, interests and outlook.

At the beginning of the present century, children were studied more systematically. In America this took the direction of behavioural studies, with emphasis upon the child's growth and development, the establishment of age norms for different kinds of behaviour and the influence of genetic and environmental factors on adjustment. European lines of research, on the other hand, in Murphy's (1949) words, 'continued to be guided by preoccupations with the great traditional questions about the mind of the child, such as characterized the work of Pestalozzi and Preyer'. This tendency was later repeated more clearly in the work of Isaacs and particularly Piaget both of whom, in their different ways, attempted to understand the nature of the intellectual processes underlying children's thinking. At the same time, other investigators directed attention to the more intangible social and emotional aspects of children's development. This work became represented explicitly in the growth of the child guidance movement which over the past seventy-five years emerged as a separate discipline with its own distinctive aims and methods and which constitutes one of the most significant features of modern child psychology.

2
Theories of personality formation

Introduction

Another notable feature of modern educational psychology is the emphasis that is given, not only to the experimental investigation of the different stages of children's development but to more general considerations of how their personalities are formed. This latter approach is represented by contemporary psychological theories of personality, as well as those of the recent past, and the purpose of this chapter is to outline the more important of these, and to discuss their implications both for the teacher and the child. From a developmental point of view, the basic questions here are, 'How does the self constitute itself in its growth?' 'How are the social and emotional qualities of children's personalities formed and what bearing do these have on their schooling and everyday life?'

It will be appreciated that it is beyond the scope of a review such as this to give detailed descriptions of all the notions and experiments about the formation of the human personality, and that they must, of necessity, be treated somewhat summarily in order to allow for a reasonable discussion of their educational significance. With this qualification, the following theories will be considered: depth or psychoanalytic theory: social-field accounts; early theories of instinct and recent advances in this field; the theory of learned drives and functional autonomy developed by G. W. Allport; factorial or structural studies, both British and American, of various personality topics in the fields of general psychology and child development.

Depth or psychoanalytic theory

The principal doctrines of the depth or psychoanalytic school of psychology are those of Freud (1915, 1923, 1927, etc.), Jung (1921, 1923, 1953, 1954) and Adler (1935, 1958), and their modern derivatives, namely, the psychology of ego-involvement and personal identity (Anna Freud, 1937, Erikson, 1950) and the psychoanalytic theory of object-relations (Klein, 1948, Fairbairn, 1952). Although there are important differences between these accounts, they have certain features in common. In the first place, they all stress the continuity of the psychic processes underlying both normal and abnormal behaviour. Second, they assume the existence in each person of an unconscious mind, believing that much of an individual's behaviour is influenced by motives he is not aware of. As Knight (1958) has pointed out, for Freud these unconscious motives consisted mainly of repressed sentiments, for Adler they were unverbalized attitudes and for Jung, unrealized potentialities. In all cases, however, they were mediated through such processes as repression, identification, sublimation, transference and so on.

Depth theorists also stress the supreme importance of the early years of childhood for the development of later personality patterns. Freudians, for example, with their concept of infantile sexuality and stages of psychosexual development, are most interested in the young child's conscious and unconscious attitudes towards his parents, believing that many adult troubles are caused initially by the deep-seated, unresolved conflicts of childhood. Adlerians, on the other hand, stress the adult's 'style of life', that is, the three major, habitual adjustments the individual has to make—to society, to sex and to work. Adjustment to society is the most important of these since it has its origins in the manner in which the adult, as a child, sought to achieve a sense of adequacy and self-confidence in his relationships with others. According to Adler's doctrine of social interest, every child has a natural capacity for being happy, friendly and secure, but these attributes develop only if he is treated properly in the early years and if the give-and-take involved in his early social relationships is able to be worked out satisfactorily and transferred to his later behaviour. Jungians likewise place great emphasis on the early experiences and environment of childhood since these, they maintain, help to determine both the adult's characteristic mode of functioning and his general attitude to life.

Over the years the above theories and their off-shoots have been subjected to considerable opposition, most of which, as Nott (1962) has pointed out, has been directed towards their concept of the unconscious, with what she calls 'its implied assault on our rational self-esteem'. Thus doubts have been cast upon the importance that Freud claimed for the unconscious motives of aggression, sex and guilt, on Jung's notion of archetypes and on Adler's views on the universal urge in man to compensate for his feelings of inferiority. Again, many critics cannot accept the ideas of depth theory on logical or scientific grounds, attacking the qualitative nature of its data and its lack of experimental verification. Eysenck's (1960) two-dimensional theory of personality organization based on the intercorrelations of objective tests and ratings may be cited here as an example of a recent attempt to make more explicit than before psychiatric notions about personality and to quantify clinical assessments in accordance with scientific methods. Mention may also be made of the findings of social psychology and field theory, both of which, as we shall see, give increasing recognition to the influence of social forces outside the family, particularly those of school and neighbourhood.

How, then, may the contributions of depth theory be assessed and what are its implications for teaching? Undoubtedly the most significant thing about it is the suggestion that children's behaviour must, if possible, be understood before it is judged and, even more important, that the explanation of many of their difficulties and problems in school and home has to be sought in the inner world of fantasy and feeling. Second, depth theory affirms that our own behaviour as adults towards children and towards each other is influenced by unconscious motives and processes in precisely the same way. Third, depth theory emphasizes, both at the conscious and unconscious levels of experience, the importance of emotional factors in learning. Thus it has shown how the child's security and adjustment constitute two of the most fundamental bases for success in school work, while conversely, conditions of maladjustment, instability and anxiety are often the most important contributory factors in cases of serious backwardness and retardation. Finally, depth theory suggests quite unequivocally that human

THEORIES OF PERSONALITY FORMATION

communication depends essentially on the quality of the personal relationship established between individuals, and that this in turn is based on the intuitive understanding, sympathy and awareness one person has for the other. There is no doubt that from an educational point of view these things form the essence of successful teaching since method itself rests on communication, and communication in its turn on the nature of relationship that exists between a teacher and his class.

Summarizing the contributions made by depth theory to the study of personality and education, note should be taken of the following:

(a) The emphasis given to unconscious mental processes in childhood and the part played by emotional factors generally in learning.

(b) The importance of pupil-teacher and parent-child relationships and the fact that normal emotional development in childhood occurs principally through these mediums.

(c) The significance for teaching of mental health concepts together with the notion of guidance as an educational aim. Two dangers here, however, must be mentioned; first, the tendency for interested but unqualified enthusiasts to continually seek psychological motivation and explanation for every aspect of children's behaviour, and second, the heartfelt desire (by the same people usually) to be assessors or interlocutors of such behaviour, so that, as Morris (1958) puts it, 'Life then becomes a stream of interpretations.' The same writer states:

> It must be emphasized that no responsible psychologist ever gives direct personal interpretations of behaviour outside a therapeutic relationship. Teaching is in some

respects necessarily a therapeutic relationship, but the therapy required is largely that of spontaneous intuitive understanding. *That* should be the goal of the education of teachers for mental health in the classroom, *not* an extensive academic knowledge of the more intricate parts of dynamic psychology, or a quack skill in discovering unconscious meanings in everyday life.

(d) Mention should also be made of the more recent psychoanalytic concept of 'personal identity' which, it is claimed, is achieved through the joint development of intelligence and inner stability within a framework of satisfying socio-cultural relationships.

As Morris (1958) has written:

Reason can only function as a decisive influence in the wise conduct of life within a personality which is not at the mercy of unconscious anxieties and identifications, but which has achieved a level of integration such that its primitive components no longer function autonomously. Such a person will not be inclined either to exploit his fellows or to be exploited by them and will be immune from compulsive love and hate. These are among the characteristics of a sense of personal identity, and they are the prerequisites for psychological freedom and the reaching of judicious decisions. That is to say they are the marks of the mature and mentally healthy person.

Social-field theories

In striking contrast to depth theory, with its emphasis on the unconscious as the chief determinant of behaviour, is the attempt of the social-field theorists to study personality as a function of environmental influences and social groups. 'Environmental' is extended in meaning here to include not merely the individual's physical and material surroundings, but the emotional and social experiences that impinge upon him as a member of a group—'circumstancia' as the Spanish philosopher Ortegay Gasset called it in describing his concept of 'mass man'. The theories that attempt to explain personality in these terms are known as (a) culture-pattern theories, as seen, for instance, in the studies of Mead (1955) and Benedict (1935) and (b) field theories, notably those of Lewin (1948), Moreno (1954) and Rogers (1942).

The idea behind culture-pattern theory is that personality differences are due to the customs, standards and ideas of different ethnic and regional groups as well as to the influence of different social and occupational subgroups within the same culture. Thus the status which people possess in such groups, the roles they play in them, their habitual mode of behaviour and, above all, their tendency to conform to the proprieties, inhibitions and sanctions of prevailing social conditions, are all examples of how the culture-pattern within which they live helps to shape the development of their personalities.

Field theories, as distinct from the foregoing, affirm that personality is not so much a function of social customs and expectations as of the interaction between the individual and social forces and pressures within the community. These are exemplified principally in such things as the demands, interests, attitudes and relations of other members of society towards one. In fact, under field theory a person is conceived largely as a set of relationships rather than as someone unique in himself. Such a view thus tends to ignore individuality and the previous life-history of the person, and to emphasize instead the significance of existing human relations within the immediate social field.

Among early investigations of the influence of human relationships in educational situations were Lewin's (1948) studies of dictatorial, laissez-faire and democratic leadership among teachers, Anderson's (1945-6) *Studies of Teachers' Classroom Personalities* and Moreno's (1954) investigations of children's friendship groupings. These enquiries were quickly followed by other studies dealing with such topics as pupil-teacher relationships, the influence of different social and emotional climates on children's learning and adjustment, the effects of different social tensions and pressures upon them, the nature of children's participative behaviour in school and class, together with studies of their attitudes, interests, fears, hopes, expectations and so on. Along with the ever-growing extension of these topics have come notable developments in research techniques of observation and measurement, the methodology of which, however, need not be detailed here since several authoritative texts are readily available for this purpose (e.g. Klein, 1956; Sprott, 1958; Evans, 1961; Stewart, 1962).

The principal effect of all these ideas and experiments has been the greatly increased recognition given to the significance of social influences in education. Thus, emphasis has been directed to the fact that teaching situations are always social situations and that children learn within the system of group relationships and shared experiences that stem from the corporate life of school and class. Fleming (1958) has recently referred to 'the comfort of recognized participation in common purposes' and this expresses the principle that school learning is predominantly social in nature.

THEORIES OF PERSONALITY FORMATION

Equally important is the knowledge that a teacher's responsibilities do not merely consist in teaching and understanding children but in being aware of all the subtle personal relationships that exist between the pupils in his class—the reciprocating groups, the stars, the isolates and so on. To this must be added the fact that a teacher's own attitude and personality affect pupils far more than 'method', so much so, in fact, that in the end personality and teaching method become indistinguishable.

From a psychological point of view, social-field theories have demonstrated the artificiality attendant upon studying personality in isolation from society. Hence, if one were to enquire of psychology how the child's self is constituted in its growth, the clear answer is that, in the social aspects of its development, the self grows and feeds on others through the images it takes into itself via play, imitation and in its dealings generally with people in different social situations.

Finally, there is the effect that social-field theories have had on other theories of personality, not least among which are those that attempt to explain behaviour in terms of certain innate, unlearned propensities, known colloquially as instincts. It is to these accounts that we must now turn our attention.

Instinct theory

There are three main bodies of work dealing with the influence of inherited tendencies on the development of personality. They are: (a) early doctrines of instinct (James, McDougall, Drever, Lloyd Morgan); (b) the findings and concepts of comparative ethology (Lorenz, Tinbergen); and (c) psychoanalytic accounts (principally the instinct theory of Freud). An excellent critical review of all these studies is provided by Fletcher (1957).

Without doubt the theory which until fairly recently exerted the greatest influence on British educationists was that of William McDougall (1908) who listed some twelve major instincts which he regarded as 'the essential springs and motive powers of all thought and action'. He defined an instinct as:

An innate disposition which determines the organism to perceive (to pay attention to) any object of a certain class, and to experience in its presence a certain emotional excitement and an impulse to action which find expression in a specific mode of behaviour in relation to that object.

On this view, instincts had three clear phases: (a) perceptual/cognitive, (b) affective/emotional and (c) active/conative.

An equally important point in McDougall's theory was that the instincts, under the influence of training and experience, were said to become organized into sentiments and so, in the words of Knight (1958), 'bring order, integration and continuity into our emotional life and make for behaviour which is consistent and predictable'.

McDougall's views had a profound effect on the writings of Nunn, Burt, Hughes and Hughes, Ross, Valentine and other psychologists in the 1920-30s. Thus Nunn (1920) spoke of instincts as 'the real springs of educational progress, both in conduct and in learning', while Burt conceived general emotionality as the central factor underlying the instinctual process. Burt (1939) regarded general emotionality as a source of mental energy which, if it failed, would result in the intellect becoming impeded

THEORIES OF PERSONALITY FORMATION

in its functioning. He asserted that many cases of backwardness and retardation resulted from some defect in the supply of the pupil's emotional energy, and he claimed to have found three types who appeared to be retarded for emotional reasons, (a) the excitable and repressed, (b) the sensitive and repressed and (c) the temperamentally apathetic.

The early theory of instinct proposed by McDougall soon ran into vehement opposition both in Britain and America. As Knight has pointed out, it was castigated because so many so-called 'innate' tendencies in children were shown to be acquired in their early years, or, as social anthropology claimed, were chiefly due to the different customs and mode of upbringing favoured by various ethnic groups. Other objections came from those who, like Allport (1937), believed that new, learned, autonomous patterns of behaviour quickly came to supplant many of the individual's inherited tendencies. Finally, instinct theory was criticized on the grounds that 'it tends to substitute abstract tendencies for concrete causes and to make its adherents blind to the evidence of learning and adjustment, not only in human but also in animal behaviour'.

Because of these criticisms, the early doctrine of instincts became unacceptable to many psychologists in the period of the late 1930s to the mid-50s. Subsequently, however, a marked revival of interest has occurred, largely through the findings of comparative ethology as evidenced in the writings of Lorenz (1952) and Tinbergen (1951). Their view is that certain instinctive patterns of behaviour emerge with the growth and maturation of the individual and are extremely important for his learning and adjustment. Furthermore, it is claimed that at particular periods in the life-history of the individual definite kinds of learning occur through the sudden ripening of various instinctive or appetitive phases. In ethology such learning is associated with what is known as the Critical Period Hypothesis. With Lorenz's geese and Tinbergen's dogs this learning happened extremely rapidly, took place only in the early years and was irreversible. Commenting on the critical period Fletcher (1957) writes:

> This is a very significant fact for our understanding of the early establishment of the 'social responses' and it is clear that if it could be shown that such critical periods occurred during the life-history of the human individual, this would constitute knowledge of the very greatest importance for social psychology and for educational theory.

Such a notion is not altogether new to psychology, however, Freud's theory of psychosexual development in childhood, James' 'periods of importance' and the readiness idea in educational psychology all being expressions of the same notion. Thus James (1892) wrote:

> If during the time of such an instinct's vivacity, objects to arouse it are met with, a *habit* of acting on them is formed, which remains when the original instinct has passed away, but if no such objects are met with, then no habit will be formed, and later on in life, when the animal meets with objects, he will fail altogether to react, as at an earlier epoch, he would instinctively have done.

The present position, then, concerning the influence of instincts on personality and learning is that while their importance is recognized, what they actually are is still controversial.

Fletcher's (1957) recent classification is illuminating here, being based on those features of human behaviour and experience that (a) have a definite, inherited neurophysiological basis, (b) an unlearned appetitive or conative element and (c) a certain sequence of activity terminating in consummatory behaviour and a definite end state. His enumeration includes: (1) *the instincts proper* (breathing, eating, sleeping, etc., general activity, bodily and mentally; sexual activity, homemaking, etc.), (2) *general instinctive tendencies* (ego-tendencies) 'brought about by the innate constitution of man coming to terms with his environment', e.g. pleasure-pain, attachment-avoidance, positive and negative ego-tendencies, (3) *secondary impulses*, viz. inhibitions and aspirations.

Another writer Tinbergen (1951) places emphasis on the neurophysiological mechanisms underlying instinctive behaviour and regards an instinct as 'a hierarchical organized nervous mechanism which is susceptible to certain primary, releasing and directing impulses of internal as well as external origin, and which responds to these impulses by co-ordinated movements that contribute to the maintenance of the individual and the species'.

However much these more recent views may differ from each other and from McDougall's theory, they all agree that instinctual behaviour is (a) extremely plastic, (b) largely dependent on processes of learning and social factors, (c) subject to intelligent control, and thus permitting great modification by the individual in accordance with his circumstances and experiences. There is also agreement over the fact that the striving-feeling aspect of instincts is their chief distinguishing feature. Some years previously both Drever and Lloyd Morgan had used the terms 'instinct-interest' and 'instinct-meaning' to refer to this striving-feeling element. Freud's term 'object-cathexis' which refers to the concentration of psychic energy towards a person or thing, has a similar connotation. The idea is that in many instinctual experiences there arise feelings of worthwhileness and significance that quickly become powerful motivators for later learning. How important it is in education to know exactly what kinds of activities and interests are likely to appeal to children in this way is so self-evident as to require no further comment here.

Similarly, the emphasis given by comparative ethology to the Critical Period Hypothesis and to the importance of the emotional aspects of the learning processes, especially in the early years, is also well-recognized. As Fletcher has written: 'This means that learning processes of fundamental importance for the formation of the individual's personality have already taken place before the child ever attends educational institutions proper'.

Healthy co-operation between home and school when the child does start attending, along with satisfactory parent-child and teacher-pupil relationships, thus paradoxically assume, under modern versions of instinct theory, great significance as contributory factors in the development of children's personalities.

Allport's theory of functional autonomy

Another theory that emphasizes, if to a lesser extent, the interaction between instinctive tendencies and environmental influences, insofar as personality structure and growth are concerned, is Allport's (1937) account of the functional autonomy of learned drives and motives.

Allport's theory is more dynamic than descriptive, that

THEORIES OF PERSONALITY FORMATION

is, it is interested mainly in human motives and in attempting to explain why children and men behave as they do. It sees personality as something essentially active, purposive and self-regulating, and as a structure that is constantly evolving and changing. In Allport's words: 'If the psychology of personality is to be more than a matter of coefficients of correlation it *must* be a dynamic psychology and seek first and foremost a sound and adequate theory of the nature of human dispositions.'

Accordingly, much early behaviour is explained in terms of simple, organic instincts or impulses which act so as to reduce tensions in the child. But soon, through learning and experience, more complex interests, attitudes, habits and values are built up and it is these that ultimately determine behaviour. Furthermore, the drives and interests acquired in this way become organized into what Allport calls psychological systems of traits.

A trait may be defined as a broad trend of behaviour. According to Allport it has more than nominal existence, however, and is akin to a generalized habit. It is dynamic, or at least determinative, and may be established empirically or statistically. Finally, though traits are only relatively independent of one another, 'In the future perhaps it may be possible to agree upon a certain magnitude of correlation below which it will be acceptable to speak of separate traits, and above which *one* trait only will be recognized. If one trait only is indicated it will presumably represent a broadly generalized disposition.' (*Psychological Theory* ed. Melvin H. Marx 'The Personality Trait' by Gordon W. Allport).

These traits, as defined by Allport, may be either active or latent, but in every case lie within the individual and behind his behaviour, which they thus serve to explain.

Other features of Allport's theory are best left to his own words:

> The dynamic psychology proposed here regards adult motives as infinitely varied, and as self-sustaining, contemporary systems, growing out of antecedent systems, but functionally independent of them. Just as a child gradually repudiates his dependence on his parents, develops a will of his own, becomes self-active and self-determining, and outlives his parents, so it is with motives. Each motive has a definite point of origin which may lie in the hypothetical instincts or more likely, in the organic tensions and diffuse innate ability. Theoretically, all adult purposes can be traced back to these seed forms in infancy. But as the individual matures, the bond is broken. The tie is historical, not functional.

A comparison of Allport's theory with that of McDougall shows that although both assume the existence of innate, primitive drives in early life, McDougall's account stresses the subsequent development of these into integrated systems of emotional habits and sentiments, whereas Allport's description favours the acquisition of new and more changeable patterns of behaviour closely linked to socio-cultural influences.

The educational implications of the two theories are also different. As Peel (1956) has indicated: 'If the instincts are taken as relatively fixed, the teacher's job is to canalize them, to adapt education to them, to find a socially acceptable substitute activity. Following Allport's theory the teacher would emphasize new learned interests'.

In actual fact, the difference in roles assigned to teachers under Allport's and McDougall's accounts is more apparent than real since both explanations suggest quite clearly that a child's personality, far from being a fixed and permanent entity, consists of many educable qualities, interests and needs that develop over and above its more primitive impulses.

Factoral or structural theories of personality

A further controversial approach to personality study is that provided by various factoral or structural theories. These have, as their rationale, not the subjective analysis of the total personality, but the empirical testing and measurement of many different psychological qualities or traits and the classification of these in terms of certain key factors or dimensions which, it is asserted, furnish the essential structure of personality.

The psychometric procedures used in these studies, along with recent developments in such techniques as the trait-composite method, pattern-tabulation and the more esoteric multivariate and hypothetico-deductive approaches will not be detailed here, several authoriative texts being available for this purpose (Eysenck 1957; Cattell 1950; 1957; Allen 1958). Space likewise does not permit discussion of the value and limitations of the numerous personality tests and inventories now available for research and diagnostic purposes. Interested readers should consult Vernon (1957), Warburton (1962) and Buros (1959) in this connection. What will be attempted, however, is a brief critique of some recent factoral theories of personality together with an assessment of their educational significance.

One of the earliest accounts was Burt's notion of the hierarchical arrangement of children's temperamental qualities which he regarded as consisting of a general factor of emotionality, bi-polar factors of extraversion-introversion and pleasure-displeasure, in addition to several other factors purporting to represent sociability, assertiveness, anger, curiosity, comfort, tenderness, fear and sorrow. This classification was similar in outline to Burt's well-known view of the structure of intellectual ability which postulated first a general integrative factor 'g' common to all tests and then, at the associative and perceptual levels of thought, various group and specific factors. Unlike his factoral studies of intelligence, however, Burt's concept of general emotionality was based on ratings which tend to be arbitrary, capricious and more unreliable than empirical test results.

Another interpretation that also made use of ratings was that of R. B. Cattell who, in keeping with the American view of the unitary nature of traits, attempted to establish the major dimensions of personality by naming some twelve primary source traits. These were conceived not merely as independent factors but as the underlying structure of behaviour that caused the observed correlations between different personality variables. In general, British investigators do not believe that Cattell's primary source factors constitute unitary source traits.

In spite of these and other differences in the British and American viewpoints, however, many factoral studies of personality reveal a number of common qualities. As Peel (1956) has indicated, extraversion-introversion usually shows up in some form or other, and the same is true of the emotional stability-instability factor. Vernon (1957), after collecting statistical studies of personality patterns in normal people, suggests that the two most pervasive dimensions are (a) dependability (i.e. the opposite of emotionality), consisting of a blend of persistence, pur-

THEORIES OF PERSONALITY FORMATION

posiveness, good character and emotional stability, and (b) sociability, characterized by those people who are friendly and co-operative and as contrasted with those who tend to be uncommunicative and unsociable.

Turning now from the normal to the abnormal, mention may be made of Eysenck's dimensional theory of personality organization based on a statistical study of the relationship between different groups of symptoms in adult psychiatric patients. Objective personality tests and inventories were combined with clinical ratings, and analysis of the data showed two relatively orthogonal clusters of items which, it was claimed, differentiated between neuroticism and psychoticism.

Symptoms characteristic of neuroticism were: anxiety, childhood problems, hysteria, unsatisfactory adjustment at adolescent, family history neurosis, depression, low energy output, bad work record, various hypochondrical symptoms. Those pertaining to psychoticism were delusions, hallucinations, mood disturbances, social withdrawal, impairment of thought or memory, family history of psychosis.

Eysenck concluded from his studies that two different continua or dimensions of personality were needed for the description of neurotic and psychotic disorders. He proceeded further, however, and showed that the symptoms making for neuroticism were themselves generated by two independent factors, emotionally on the one hand, and the familiar extraversion-introversion dichotomy on the other. In consequence, two major syndromes were accounted for—extraverted neurotics and introverted neurotics or dysthmics.

Significant off-shoots from Cattell's and Eysenck's studies have been (a) the development of many ingenious devices for improving the validity of personality test data and the methods of statistical analysis, and (b) the application of these procedures to the scientific investigation of children's personalities. Notable among the former are the new hypothetico-deductive techniques of construct validity[1] and multidimensional testing, together with improved methods for estimating the significance of factors and the calculation of individual factor scores. Of the application of these procedures to the study of children's personalities, mention may be made of Cattell's (1957) studies of source-trait structure in children aged 4-14 years; the investigations of Lynn (1960, 1961) into the relationship of neuroticism and extraversion to intelligence and educational achievement; Thorpe's (1960) enquiries into neuroticism in children; and Eysenck's (1960) account of the contribution of modern behaviourist learning theory to the study of children's moral development.

But against these advances made by the factor analytic approach, a measure of criticism must be set. This is directed mainly to the following: (a) the limitations of trait-measurement procedures which, it is alleged, abstract personality and tend to cross-section it at the expense of dynamic tendencies, (b) the extreme empiricism of some personality tests and inventories and the fact that no account is taken of the meaning or significance the question in such tests might have for the individual, (c) the artificiality of the factors themselves which, it is held,

---

[1] The means whereby rational tests, i.e. tests developed on the basis of a theory or construct are validated; it consists essentially of the setting up of specific testable hypotheses for the purpose of determining whether the constructs are tenable or untenable. See Eysenck, H. J.: *The Dynamics of Anxiety and Hysteria*, Chapter 8, p. 261; and Cronbach, L. J. and Meehl, P. E.: 'Construct Validity in Psychological Tests', *Psychol. Bull.* 1955, 52, pp. 281-302.

are nothing more than statistical artefacts lacking any kind of psychological reality.

In reply to these criticisms factorists claim, first, that psychology is not yet in a position to deal adequately with the whole nebulous complexity of the 'total personality', and in consequence, restricted, part-function theories and experiments of the more outstanding social and emotional attributes are needed. Second, so far as the reality of the factors are concerned, all scientific concepts being abstracted generalizations have no 'real' existence as such. Psychological factors fall within this category but nevertheless provide useful classifications of many diverse personal qualities for selection, diagnostic and guidance purposes as well as indicating other problems and hypotheses for experimental investigation. Finally, to those critics who object to the extreme empiricism of the factoral approach, the answer is that if the psychological measurement of personality is to have any meaning or validity at all—in education, industry, clinical work and elsewhere —it must become even more explicit in its quantification procedures and techniques of statistical control. For these now constitute the accepted principles of scientific method to which all branches of applied psychology and experimental education must adhere if they are to add to their already considerable knowledge of human behaviour and experience.

Conclusions

The concept of guidance in educational psychology implies among other things the systematic study of the social and emotional aspects of development in children. It is here that personality theory has a distinctive contribution to make in the different explanations it offers of the principal features of this development and human behaviour generally. All that remains for us to do now is to consider the values, limitations and points of agreement contained in the various approaches we have so far discussed.

The first and most obvious thing personality theories have in common is the emphasis they give to the importance of the individual's interaction with the social environment. Thus Adler's doctrine of social interest, the insistence of Allport on the contemporary circumstances of life, the early establishment of the social responses suggested by modern instinct theory, the ubiquity of the extraversion-introversion factor revealed by empirical studies—all these indicate that personality is something predominantly social in nature, that no man is an island and can 'go it' alone. But what do we mean by the social, the man-world relation, the organism-environmental field? There is little doubt that we would be able to investigate it technically if we knew what it was. But what?— something biological, inter-personal and identifiable in time-space?

The same hesitancy arises in connection with our wholehearted acceptance of psychoanalytic accounts of personality, for the educational value of these theories lies not in their notions of the unconscious or the mechanisms of defence, but in the emphasis they attach to mental health concepts and emotional factors in learning and teaching— eminently acceptable ideas that can be postulated, however, without having to assume the existence of hidden, pocketed-off inner structures.

A similar denial must be given to certain features of modern instinct theory, though the emphasis these accounts place on the maturational aspects of development, the appetitive phases of childhood, and the fact that there are optimal times for the acquisition of certain basic habits and skills, are of great significance both for teaching and individual development.

Finally, the chief value of factorial theories of personality, as distinct from more subjective interpretations, lies in their making explicit what appear to be the essential dimensions or attributes of behaviour that are relevant to educational and vocational success. Though factorial investigations tend to be more restricted in their methods than others, they nevertheless seem the only logical and workable approach to the study of personality at present.

But whether a person's conduct is conceived in terms of certain specified categories of behaviour or as a function of social forces, personal inter-relationships, or the unconscious, the aim of personality theory is always the same, namely, to attain to a generalized form of human behaviour that also permits the more accurate description of individual differences. To this end all personality theories contribute. Out of their manifold differences a unification of principles may ultimately emerge that will be helpful in providing not only a better understanding of behaviour, particularly in its social and emotional aspects, but also in relation to the nature of the learning process. Of all the problems in educational psychology, none is more complex than the way children's behaviour is modified through their educational experiences and training. Many theories and experiments have been advanced to explain how learning occurs and it is to these that we must now direct our attention.

3
The psychology of learning

The ideas and experiments that have influenced the study of learning over the past hundred years or so may be conveniently summarized as follows:

The doctrine of Associationism as propounded by Thomas Brown, James Mill and Alexander Bain in the nineteenth century and around which all psychological problems revolved prior to the influence of Evolutionism.

The theory of evolution as exemplified in Galton's studies and in Spencer's 'developmental hypothesis', both with their emphasis on the individual's stages of natural growth in learning and adaptation.

The experiments of Ebbinghaus and his co-workers at Breslau in the 1880's *on memory* and other associative processes.

Neurological and physiological studies, particularly Sherrington's investigations into the motor reflexes and the work of the Russians, Pavlov and Bekhterev, on conditioning.

Thorndike's animal experiments in America on trial-and-error learning and, in conjunction with R. S. Woodworth, his enquiries into the nature of the transfer of training.

The subsequent development, again in America, of *the Behaviourist School of psychology* under the influence of John B. Watson in the period 1909-1919.
The work of the early Gestalt psychologists in Germany—Wertheimer, Koffka and Kohler—on *problem-solving and insightful learning*.

Associationism

Early psychological theories of learning had as their underlying theme the celebrated doctrine of Associationism. This has been described by Murphy (1949) as follows:

> Associationism is the doctrine that we connect things in memory, in thought, and in all mental life, simply because they were connected in our original experience with them; and since our first encounters with things are by means of our senses, the associationist maintains that all the complexity of mental life is reducible to sense impressions the elementary components of consciousness, as connected in experience (p. 26).

This notion of mental connections or linkages being formed from elementary sense impressions from which more complex perceptions, feelings and thoughts were developed was also intended to explain the learning process. Under Associationism, ideas, facts and other things were supposed to be learned in accordance with certain laws which purported to explain exactly how such experiences became ordered and related to one another and established in mind and action. The laws were those of similarity, contrast and contiguity and were first described in Aristotle's *De Anima* (1959)[1]. One idea recalls another said Aristotle, the recall being easier if the ideas are of a similar kind, close together in time and place or in contrast to one another.

Aristotle's notions about learning were revived and brought into British psychology by Hobbes (1651) who emphasized sensation as the source of our ideas, and differentiated between free and controlled associations. Hobbe's views were extended by Hume (1739) and Hartley (1749) in whose hands Associationism became the means of dissecting and describing every conceivable kind of experience. Indeed, British psychology in the eighteenth century was completely dominated by this approach and its effects were carried over into the early nineteenth century and into other countries, especially Germany, with Herbart's notion of dynamic tendencies.

In Britain itself the doctrine was developed still further by Thomas Brown (1820) who introduced the 'secondary' laws of Association (or 'suggestion' as he called them), the 'primary' laws being those that have already been mentioned—similarity, contrast and contiguity. The secondary laws, nine in number, have been summarized by Murphy (1949) in the following way:

1. *The relative duration of the original sensations*: 'The longer we dwell on objects, the more fully do we rely on our future remembrances of them'.

2. *Their relative liveliness*: 'The parts of a train appear to be more closely and firmly associated as the original feelings have been more lively'.

[1] Aristotle, 384-322 B.C. *'Aristotle's "De Anima" in the version of William of Moerbeke and the commentary of St. Thomas Aquinas'*. Trans by Kenelm Foster and Silvester Humphries, London, Routledge and Kegan Paul, 1954.

3. *Relative frequency*: 'The parts of any train are more readily suggested in proportion as they have been more fully renewed'.

4. *Relative recency*: 'Events which happened a few hours before are remembered when there is a total forgetfulness of what happened a few days before'.

5. *The coexistence in the past with fewer alternative associates*: 'The song which we have never heard but from one person can scarcely be heard again by us without recalling that person to our memory'.

6. *Constitutional differences between individuals modify the primary laws*: They give 'greater proportional vigour to one set of tendencies of suggestion than to another'

7. *Variations in the same individual*, 'according to the varying emotion of the hour'.

8. *Temporary diversities of state*, as in intoxication, delirium or ill-health.

9. *Prior habits of life and thought*: the influence of ingrown tendencies upon any given situation, however new or irrelevant the experience may be.

Brown's principal contribution was thus an attempt to analyse, by means of the above laws, the many factors that appear to determine the course of associations. That he emphasized emotional and constitutional factors was also significant for the study of individual differences. Important though his work was, however, it was James Mill (1829) and Alexander Bain (1855, 1859) who gave Associationism its most rigorous interpretation.

Bain's approach was through a study of the physical basis of mind and he propounded an Associationism based on the most detailed and elaborate physiological findings. The sense organs, sensory and motor nerves, brains and muscles were all considered in detail. As Brett (1951) writes:

> He dispensed entirely with any preliminary assumption either of a soul or a sensorium, or unifying agency; he preferred to deal solely in nerve-currents; the repetition of those currents and their association, in all degrees of complexity, are for Bain the real explanation of mental processes. For taking the nerves and the brain as an organic unity, Bain evolves from them the elementary states of mind—viz. instinctive muscular movements and the processes of the special senses. Motion, sensation and instinct together form the basis of the developed life of conscious beings, for consciousness is a unity in which may be distinguished as typical forms, feeling, willing and thinking. The first phase of cognition is the act of discriminating, with which stand closely connected the consciousness of agreement and the power of retention. The two latter are forms of association, and in explaining them Bain restates with remarkable fullness and completeness the whole doctrine of Associationism (pp. 443-444).

Thus, in describing the process of agreement, or similarity, in *Mind and Body* (1847) Bain writes:

> Looking at a cathedral, we readily bring to mind other cathedrals; hearing an anecdote, we are almost sure to recall some one similar. Our reason essentially consists in using an old fact in new circumstances, through the power of discerning the agreement; we have sown one field and seen it grow, and we repeat the process in another field. . . . When we have anything new to learn, as a new piece of music, or a new proposition in Euclid, we fall back upon our previously formed combinations, musical or geometrical, as far as they will

apply, and merely tack certain of them together in correspondence with the new case. The method of acquiring by patchwork sets in early, and predominates increasingly (p. 87).

Similarly, in outlining the mechanism of retention Bain says:

. . . when I see a written word and, as a result of my education pronounce it orally, the power (of retention) lies in a series of definite groupings or connections of nerve-currents in the nerve and centres of the eye, with currents in motor nerves proceeding to the chest, larynx and mouth; and these groupings or connections are affected by definite growths at certain proper or convenient cell crossings (p. 91).

During his life Bain's writings achieved tremendous popularity and although the Associationism he had so elaborately proclaimed gradually succumbed to the rising wave of Evolutionism on the one hand and the accusing finger of philosophical idealism on the other, his work continued to influence the psychology of learning and is, as Hearnshaw (1964) has pointed out, one of the major foundation stones of contemporary theories. And although, too, Associationism in its classical form may be said to have died with Bain, its central ideas did not wholly disappear but, on the contrary, continued to contribute to later theories of conditioning, memory and learning. As Gardner Murphy (1949) has said of its continuing influence:

. . . despite its official departure, coroner's inquest, and interment, it has gone cheerfully forward, and has in fact been able not only to maintain its own life, but to give life to many a psychological movement. Thus it inspired many of the early labours of Janet, Freud and Jung; thus it coloured early work on the conditioned response; thus it served as guide through the laborious studies of learning by Thorndike and others; and thus, though serving as whipping boy for other doctrines, it has become toughened in the process and reappeared in ever-new systematic form. Guthrie holds that Associationism is the only theory of learning that has ever been proposed; and while there is no need to discuss this paradox, it shows how unwilling the associationists are to agree to their own death sentence.

Evolutionism

In the same year as the publication of Bain's *The Emotions and the Will* (1859) there appeared Charles Darwin's *The Origin of Species*; and Evolutionism, which had always been one of the great recurrent themes in the history of thought, suddenly and irrevocably changed the whole pattern, of psychology in Britain. Associationism, for years the established orthodoxy, was attacked not only by the concepts of heredity development and continuous variation and adaptation, but also by the devastating criticism of James Ward (1886) and the Anglo-Hegelians Bradley (1935) and Green (1885) all of whom in their different ways insisted on the essential unity of mind. The changed point of view had already been evident in Spencer's 'developmental hypothesis' with its emphasis on the differentiation and integration of mental processes and the functions these serve in adjusting the individual to his surroundings. The studies of Galton and Sully were further expressions of these ideas, while Ward's assault on Associationism in his Encylopaedia Britannica article in 1886, and Bradley's eloquent condemnation of its tenets in *Mind* may be cited as other instances of the reverberent opposition that was now being shown towards

THE PSYCHOLOGY OF LEARNING

the old doctrine. The inevitable result of these ideas spelt death for Associationism as a system of explaining psychological experiences through the juxtaposition of sensory impressions. Evolutionism, and not Associationism. thus became the new focal point in British psychology and the greatest single factor in its subsequent development.

Ebbinghaus's memory experiments

Another important influence on the study of learning in the late nineteenth century consisted of Ebbinghaus's memory experiments which were carried out at Breslau in the 1880's. These studies were the first systematic experimental investigations of the learning processes and they set a new direction for psychology both in the development of techniques for measuring psychological processes and in the control of error variables in experimental situations. They also reflected the new experimentalism that was sweeping everything before it in Germany at this time— a movement that had started with the appearance of Wundt's *Principles of Physiological Psychology* in 1873-74, the founding of his psychological laboratory at Leipzig in 1879 and his subsequent experiments into the psychophysiology of the senses, his reaction time studies and his analysis of association.

It is interesting to note that the development of experimental psychology under Wundt was something peculiarly German, British psychology tending to adhere to its evolutionary and comparative approach, at least, until Galton revealed the advantages of combining it with statistical and experimental methods. There is no denying, however, the vigour and enthusiasm of the German movement in

1900 which has been described by Gardner Murphy (1949) in the following words:

> Wundt at Leipzig, at sixty-eight going strong, and delving into folk psychology as he kept an eye on the young experimentalists; Ebbinghaus and Breslau, ardent associationist, concerned with memory and with intelligence and its testing; G. E. Muller at Gottingen, likewise indefatigable student of memory, dean of psychophysics; Stumph at Berlin, experimental analyst of music; Stern at Hamburg, who was destined soon to create a great new place for child psychology and for psychological applications to law and industry; Kulpe and Wurzburg, about to launch a new experimental movement dealing with attitudes and thought-processes. Everywhere the new experimentalism could be seen creeping into education, too, and into psychiatry . . . over the border, in Austria, the former priest Brentano, who saw in psychology the study of psychological acts rather than of states; and sitting behind his patient's couch, the thoughtful physician Sigmund Freud, for whom dark and unspeakable things were becoming both clear and communicable.

In setting out to measure memory Ebbinghaus first constructed nonsense syllables in order to get rid of errors of a qualitative kind which otherwise would have arisen through the use of meaningful material; he then proceeded to eliminate quantitative variables by using the probable error technique. The principal problems he investigated in this way consisted of the measurement of memory span and the study of overlearning by the 'saving method', that is, by measuring the amount of work needed to relearn. Ebbinghaus also made a quantitative examination of forgetting which led to his famous 'curve of forgetting' (the general form of which still holds) consisting of an initial drop gradually becoming less steep. Another problem he studied concerned the most effective distribution of working time in which it was shown that 'spaced' repetition is preferable to continuous repetition. Finally, Ebbinghaus studied the form of associations other than those suggested by Hartley.

The immediate effect of all these studies was that for the next two decades psychological research into learning and memory was inspired and guided by Ebbinghaus's concepts and methods. One development, for example, was the demonstration that 'whole' learning is better than 'part' learning, that is to say, long passages are remembered better if they are read straight through instead of being broken down into short passages and then pieced together again. Another study showed the usefulness of the 'paired associates' method in serial learning. Even more significant psychologically, however, was the fact that all these investigations showed clearly that memory was not a unitary process, a matter of simple associations, but that different tasks require different kinds of learning—as Bartlett's study of remembering and other investigations have since shown.

Neurological and physiological studies

The psychology of learning was also influenced by advances in neurological and physiological studies which occurred in the latter half of the nineteenth century and the beginning of the twentieth. The most important of these researches were: (a) studies of the structure and function of nerve cells, leading to the development of neurone theory, now thoroughly substantiated, and according to which nerve cells are independent anatomically but connected physiologically at junction points or synapses, thus suggesting a theory of learning in terms of synaptic modification, (Cajal) and (Waldeyer); (b) Sherrington's experimental studies of motor reflexes and his measurements of the processes of summation, facilitation and inhibition, and their relations to synaptic functioning; (c) the methods and results of the Russian physiologists Pavlov and Bekhterev on the conditioned response which, although not a new idea in psychology, came to be regarded both as an explanatory principle of behaviour and the basic unit of learning and habit-formation.

The effect of these investigations was that psychological studies of association, perception and learning became much more objective and systematized than they had been in the past. Psychologists now started to think seriously in neurological and physiological concepts and to realize the extraordinary importance of the nervous system and the synapses and their organization in the study of psychological phenomena. Indeed, the possibility of constructing a theory of general behaviour based largely on physiological data provoked much thought and discussion and eventually led to the traditional laws of association being re-stated in stimulus-response relationships. That greater emphasis came to be placed on objective behaviour studies and quantitative methods of experimentation generally is a further example of the influence of these early neurological studies on the development of the psychology of learning.

Thorndike's animal experiments

Of immense importance also at the turn of the century

THE PSYCHOLOGY OF LEARNING

were Thorndike's animal studies of 'trial-and-error' learning and (in conjunction with R. S. Woodworth) his experiments on the problem of the transfer of training. The principal conclusion that Thorndike drew from his animal studies was that learning depended not on insight or understanding but on random, trial-and-error activities in the course of which the correct actions or responses appeared, albeit fortuitously, but which, through repeated practice became progressively 'stamped in', that is, learned, by their own satisfying consequences. For Thorndike the functional units in learning were what he called bonds or connections, arbitrarily established between stimuli and responses and which, through exercise and reward, became strengthened and organized into complex systems of behaviour.

The results of Thorndike's animal studies were expressed in his famous laws of learning which were natural developments of the traditional principles of association and were called (1) the law of exercise or habit-formation, and (2) the law of effect. The law of exercise, under which were included the old associationist ideas of frequency, recency and intensity, stated that bonds or connections between stimuli and responses were strengthened by use and weakened by disuse. The law of effect was merely a restatement of the principle of psychological hedonism and held that successful or satisfying responses led to a strengthening of learning bonds, while conversely, unsatisfying or annoying responses resulted in failure and a tendency for the bonds to be weakened and rendered less likely to appear again in the future.

Gardner Murphy (1949) states: 'Satisfaction and annoyance were conceived in terms of synaptic functions; when a pathway was ready to conduct, the process of conduction was satisfying, while annoyance might result either from the failure of a ready pathway to conduct or from the forced conduction of an unready pathway.'

Thorndike himself describes the process as follows:

> It is a fundamental law of mental life that if a mental state or bodily act is made to follow or accompany a certain situation with resulting satisfaction it will tend to go on with that situation in the future. The applications of the law to teaching are comprised in the simple and obvious, but too commonly neglected rules. Put together what you wish to have to go together. Reward good impulses. Conversely; keep apart what you wish to have separate. Let undesirable impulses bring discomfort.

Both the law of exercise and the law of effect have been criticized as being too simple and mechanical an explanation of human learning because they do not make sufficient allowance for the individual's own attitudes, interests and intention in learning situations. While this criticism is justified, it is nevertheless true to say that the law of exercise is a most useful explanatory principle, showing how, under appropriate conditions, many simple skills and habits are acquired. The law of effect likewise helps to explain why behaviour that is satisfying or rewarding tends to be retained in the individual and why other behaviour devoid of success and satisfaction does not usually persist.

Another problem that was studied extensively by Thorndike and also by R. S. Woodworth, was the transfer of training—that is, whether repeated practice and improvement in certain tasks lead to increased efficiency in other skills and activities. William James in the 1890s and W. F. Dearborn in 1910 were among other early investigators of this problem, studying transfer effects resulting from memory training.

Until Thorndike and Woodworth's investigation of this problem the time-honoured doctrine of formal discipline had long taught that hard work and study bestowed great and lasting benefits upon the mind, principally in the form of improvements in the powers of concentration, persistence, judgment, memory and other mental functions. The doctrine had also maintained that certain academic studies, especially those that were difficult to master, would give to the individual the gifts of a disciplined mind and a strengthened character; and this is still believed to be the essential value to be derived from the study of certain academic subjects. Mathematics, for instance, is regarded by many as the subject par excellence for improving reasoning ability, while Latin is believed to develop a general language ability.

The evidence of Thorndike and Woodworth, based on their studies of school learning, showed clearly that transfer effects from specialized training were negligible, and that the repeated exercise of intelligence, memory, attention and other functions in some particular subject or activity would not be inevitably followed by a general improvement in the function itself. On the contrary, transfer as such appeared to be due to what Thorndike and Woodworth called 'identical elements', that is specific habits and attitudes, methods of work, training material and rules of procedure that were involved in the learning activities; and the conclusion they came to was that transfer of training occurred through such identical elements, namely, through alterations taking place in specific bonds or connections, rather than by means of generalized transfer. This notion of transfer in terms of mechanical linkage between similar activities was again criticized as being altogether too restricted a view of learning since it did not take account of personal factors like interest, co-operation, intelligence and drive. Further criticism was given by C. H. Judd who stated that any improvement in one particular function resulting from training in another depended not on the transfer of identical elements as Thorndike and Woodworth had suggested, but on the elements themselves becoming generalized experiences which carried over to other functions. There is, however, no essential difference between these views, for, as Garrett (1959) has pointed out:

> The value of Latin as an aid in learning French depends upon the 'identical elements' in the two languages, as well as upon the similarity in general form and syntax which they possess in common with English. Common attitudes and techniques are best abstracted from a variety of experiences when there are identical bonds running through them all. The most common bond is language; others are everyday information, similarity of method or procedure, and plan of attack. Such connections as these supply the identical elements as well as the more abstract principles upon which transfer depends.

The general position concerning transfer, therefore, may be summarized by saying that although transfer of training is an established fact, the gains are nowhere as great as was formerly supposed. Thorndike's studies revealed that while the learning of simple motor skills and some school subjects showed greater improvements than others, the transfer effects were usually extraordinarily low. Moreover, when gains did occur, they appeared to depend more on specific teaching methods and the general intellectual ability and motives of the learners, rather than on any disciplinary virtues inherent in the actual subjects. In other words, given good teaching and high intelligence, training in almost anything will develop specific habits, attitudes, skills and techniques of work which will effectively transfer to other activities. On the other hand, however, complex psychological functions like perception, memory and reasoning processes do not appear to be capable of direct training and transfer—unless they are conceived in terms of highly specific habits and skills acquired or otherwise learned by the individual and similar to those that have just been mentioned.

The influence of E. I. Thorndike on educational psychology both in America and Britain is so well known that little need be added to what has already been written about it. From 1900 onwards his ideas and experiments on the acquisition of skill, trial-and-error learning and the transfer of training were discussed and repeated by psychologists everywhere. They had a profound and stimulating effect on J. B. Watson (1928) and the development of the behaviourist system of psychology in the period 1909-1919; they also contributed greatly to the formulation of later behaviourist theories of learning conceived in terms of stimulus-response relationships, of which Hull's theory of reinforcement based on the fact of conditioning and Thorndike's law of effect, is undoubtedly our best example at the present time.

Watson and Behaviourism

At the beginning of the twentieth century experimental psychology in America, like its counterpart in Germany,

THE PSYCHOLOGY OF LEARNING

was concerned mainly with the study of conscious experience—with understanding man's sensations, feelings, memories and thoughts—and in attempting to analyse these into their basic components. Under the influence of J. B. Watson (1878-1958), however, all this changed and instead of dealing with the analysis and synthesis of mental states and processes, American psychology became sharply orientated towards the study of objective behaviour, with a strong emphasis on the practical usefulness of its results.

Watson's objection to traditional psychology was that its data, being derived mainly from introspection, were not objectively verifiable and as such not scientifically valid or serviceable. For these reasons he broke with current theories and terminology and attempted to make a fresh start for psychology by establishing it as 'that division of natural science which takes human behaviour —the doings and sayings, both learned and unlearned, of people as its subject matter. It is the study of what people do from even before birth until death' (p. 4).

The elements of behaviour in the new science were regarded as consisting of different reactions or 'responses' to a variety of objects or situations called 'stimuli'. The stimulus-response or S-R connections thus formed constituted the basis of all Watson's studies which had, as their goal, 'the ascertaining of such data and laws that, given the stimulus, psychology can predict what the response will be; or, on the other hand, given the response, it can specify the nature of the effective stimulus' (p. 10).

Watson believed that many of the S-R connections we possess are nothing more than simple, inborn reflexes such as sneezing, coughing and the familiar phenomena of knee-jerk and eye-blink. But he also held that much of our behaviour consists of responses that are learned through the process of conditioning. Conditioning occurs when a response is elicited through constant and frequent association with a stimulus other than its natural or original one. The following examples from the works of Pavlov and Watson explain how this kind of learning takes place. In one of Pavlov's experiments a dog was made to salivate at the sound of a bell, the sound being produced at exactly the same time as food was presented to the dog. Eventually, the sound alone was sufficient to cause salivation, i.e. the response 'salivating' had become conditioned to the new stimulus 'bell'. In Watson's experiment, a child was playing happily and fearlessly with a pet white rat when Watson made a sudden loud noise behind it with a hammer. The child, being startled, fell over, cried and crawled away as fast as he could. This experiment was repeated until soon the appearance of the pet by itself brought about the fear reaction in the child. In both of these experiments it may be seen that conditioning occurred through the frequent repetition of new stimuli with the original S-R connections—the sound of the bell in the case of the dog's salivation and the sudden loud noise in the case of the child's apprehension.

From these experiments Watson concluded that the process of conditioning led to the development of new S-R connections and that these formed the basis of practically all complex human learning—intellectual habits and skills, social and emotional behaviour, the acquisition of knowledge itself—all being explained in this way. Conditioning, however, was not the whole answer and Watson brought forward two further principles to explain learning —frequency and recency—which, as we already know, were subheadings under the old associationist law of exercise proposed by Thorndike some years earlier. The principle of frequency stated that the more frequent a response is made to a given stimulus, the more likely will that response be made to the stimulus again. Similarly, the principle of recency held that the more recent the response, the more likely we are to make it again.

These two laws, together with the fact of conditioning, were sufficient to explain the nature of learning to the behaviourists. It may thus be seen that such a theory made little or no concession to the inheritance of mental abilities or traits, so dear to the heart of traditional psychology. On the contrary, by confining itself entirely to the study of objective behaviour and with supreme faith in the power of learning, it led to the belief that there was no limit to what man, properly conditioned, might become. But, as Hill (1963) has pointed out:

> In many respects, 'objective behaviour' meant nothing more than the study of the movement of muscles. Speech, for example, was seen as the movement of the throat muscles, thought as subvocal speech, feeling and emotion as movement of the muscles of the gut, and so on. This, of course, was not the whole explanation since all behaviour tends to involve the whole body. When we think, we may pace the floor or furrow our brows. We announce our opinions with smiles or waves of the arm as well as with words. We cannot therefore really say that emotions are responses of the gut or that thinking is made up of vocal responses. Everything we think, feel, say or do involves the activity of, to varying degrees, the entire body. This is probably the most fundamental credo of Behaviourism.

How, then, may Watson and Behaviourism be evaluated? In the first place, Watson did not carry his experiments and theorizing far enough and was inclined to be somewhat cavalier in the matter of logical thoroughness when it came to explaining the complexity of human behaviour and development in terms of a few simple principles. He made no attempt, for example, to determine the relationship between conditioning, frequency and recency. On the other hand, by rejecting body-mind distinctions and emphasizing the study of overt behaviour, Watson did much to free psychology from subjectivism and to make it a scientific and objective subject of study. Finally, by showing a preference for stimulus-response analysis and by concentrating on learning as the central topic of psychology, Watson, more than any other man, laid the foundations for the subsequent development of more comprehensive theories of behaviour and learning. That all contemporary American learning theories are, generally speaking, behaviourist, is due in no small measure to Watson's trail-blazing.

Learning by insight

Another theory of learning completely different from behaviourist and associationist accounts was that which originated in Germany in the first two decades of the present century as part of a vigorous movement that came to be known as Gestalt psychology—the psychology of form.

The Gestalt movement was strongly opposed to attempts to analyse consciousness into what was thought to be its constituent elements, as well as to other descriptions of mind based on stimulus-response relationships. It maintained instead that any complex experience has a certain structure and wholeness to it—a unique quality that is dependent, not on the aggregation of the separate entities in the experience itself, but on the organization of these into a form or configuration quite different from that given by the sum of the discrete parts, yet within itself perfectly meaningful, satisfying and complete.

The notion that the total character of an experience is something different from that given by an analysis or aggregation of its various elements had been clearly recognized in the nineteenth century by Thomas Brown, Hartley, J. S. Mill and Alexander Bain, in spite of their frank acceptance of associationist theory; and above all, by William James, who regarded consciousness as 'nothing jointed' or 'chopped up in bits' but as something continuously flowing and changing, like a river or a stream, so that 'however complex the object may be, the thought of it is one undivided state of consciousness' (Principles, Vol. I, p. 276). James also wrote: 'Whatever things are thought in relation are thought from the outset in a unity, in a single pulse of subjectivity, a single psychoses, feeling or state of mind' (p. 278). Decrying still further the attempts of the associationists to reduce human experience to a series of fixed components James said:

> No doubt it is often convenient to formulate the mental facts in an atomistic sort of way, and to treat the higher stages of consciousness as if they were all built out of unchanging simple ideas which 'pass and turn again'. It is convenient often to treat curves as if they were composed of small straight lines, and electricity and nerve force as if they were fluids. But in the one case as in the other we must never forget that we are talking symbolically and that there is nothing in nature to answer our words. A permanently existing 'Idea' which makes its appearance before the footlights of conscious-

ness at periodical intervals is as mythological entity as the Jack of Spades (*A Textbook of Psychology*, p. 157).

While James conceived personal consciousness as something continuous and incessantly changing, other psychologists believed that much human behaviour could be better explained by studying the matter in which the elements that seemed to make up any individual experience became organized into a complete and meaningful whole. This point of view was held by two of the early forerunners of Gestalt psychology in Germany—Ernst Mach and Christian von Ehrenfels. In *Contributions to the Analysis of Sensations* (1886) Mach noted that the arrangement of dots or lines into geometrical figures gave rise to what he called 'sensations of space' (e.g. triangularity). These sensations did not really correspond to the dots or lines but were dependent upon certain internal or subjective relations existing between them—relations which, though not physically present in any particular geometrical figure, nevertheless formed an integral part of the individual's perception of it and, in consequence, gave the whole experience a stability and structure it would not otherwise possess. The same conclusion was reached by von Ehrenfels who used the term 'Gestaltqualitat' to denote the qualities of organized wholes over and above their original elements—'form' qualities that were brought about by an integration of the separate sensations and perceptions in any single experience into something completely new.

But what exactly were these 'form qualities' and how did they become related to other aspects already present in a particular experience? These questions remained unanswered until the investigations of three other German psychologists (Wertheimer, Koffka and Kohler) made clear the general principles and conditions relating not only to the structure or organization of experience, but to the development of an entirely new theory of learning based upon it.

The first of these studies was Wertheimer's investigation in 1912 into the phi-phenomenon[1] which he regarded as a complete perceptual experience in itself, not reducible to isolated sensations or, as Lotze (1881) had previously maintained, to the successive stimulation of sensory points or 'local signs' which, through learning and experience, gradually built up to give the individual his ideas of space. This view was rejected by Wertheimer who asserted instead that in all perceptions there were unique characteristics of structure which did not belong to an amalgamation of single sensations or to any serial arrangement of their stimuli.

As a further protest against such elementarism Wertheimer formulated two basic laws concerning the relationship of parts to a whole. The first was called the law of membership character. According to this, the constituent aspects or attributes of any structure whole (e.g. notes in a melody, colours in a painting, lines in a drawing, words in a poem) possess qualities, values and meaning which are dependent solely upon their place and relationship within the total situation. The second law was known as 'Pragnanz' or goodness of form, and was said to result from certain types of inner relationship giving stability

[1] The phi-phenomenon was a term used by Wertheimer to denote the perception of motion or apparent movement brought about by the rapid presentation of stimuli in different but close positions. 'Still' pictures shown quickly and successively produce the phenomenon.

and intelligible organization to the whole. Some of the factors that make for clarity of form are similarity and proximity of the elements and the ability of the learner to use his experience to structure and re-arrange these, and by so doing to discover clearer and more meaningful relationships or insights into the problem at hand.

The early studies of Wertheimer were quickly extended and systematized by Kohler's demonstrations of insightful learning by chimpanzees at Teneriffe during World War I. These experiments were reported during the years 1917-21, and about the same time Koffka published his educational psychology in *The Growth of the Mind* which, in keeping with Gestalt theory as a psychology of thinking, was based on the thesis that learning proceeds mainly by the apprehension of order and meaning rather than, as Thorndike had maintained, by blind, trial-and-error methods. Gardner Murphy (1949) has expressed the Gestalt viewpoint as follows:

> It was the process of thinking which intrigued Kohler in his comparison of man with apes. It was thinking which intrigued Koffka as he first ventured to conceive educational psychology as the successive realization of levels of complexity, growing out of the capacity of the individual to move ever toward higher integrations rather than simply to acquire piecemeal one new response at a time.

The educational implications of modern versions of Gestalt theory, namely, the need for the learner to be active in organizing his thoughts and experiences, and the teacher's function in providing the necessary conditions for clear insights to occur, are so well known that they need not be discussed here. That adherence to these tenets is likewise not incompatible with the need for adequate practice in the learning of any skill, as contemporary behaviourist accounts suggest, is also recognized. Both kinds of theory have their part to play in education and thus, in their different ways, have helped to contribute to our understanding of the learning process, particularly in its intellectual aspects.

4
Mental testing and measurement

The purpose of this chapter is to provide a review of the antecedents of modern psychological tests. Such tests are currently employed in the solution of a wide range of practical educational problems, and a knowledge of their origins will aid in the understanding of present day tests and at the same time show how this relatively young branch of educational psychology is currently employed as an aid to the assessment of children's learning and progress in school.

The function of psychological tests is to measure individual differences in mental ability and early interest in the field centred on the classification of the feebleminded and insane. One immediate problem which accompanied the more humane attitude of the mid-nineteenth century towards the individual was the need to measure their abilities and, if possible to discriminate between them.

Early interest in the classification of the feebleminded

The first explicit statement of this distinction was that of the French Physician, Esquirol, who, in 1838, pointed out that there were many degrees of feeblemindedness, varying from high grade defectives to low grade idiots. Among the tests considered by Esquirol for the purpose of classifying the varieties of feeblemindedness were different kinds of physical measures, including the size and shape of the skull—a technique which the Italian Lombroso used extensively but erroneously towards the end of the nineteenth century, in an attempt to identify the congenital criminal type. But the most dependable criterion of intellectual level considered by Esquirol, was that of language and on this basis he distinguished two grades of imbecility and three grades of idiocy. In the highest grade of imbecility, Esquirol found that speech was used readily and easily, whilst in the lowest grade speech was more difficult and the use of vocabulary severely restricted.

It is interesting to note that verbal ability enters largely into modern concepts of intelligence and that many present day intelligence tests, in keeping with Esquirol's findings, are mainly linguistic in content.

Another pioneer in the testing and training of the feebleminded was E. Seguin who rejected the prevalent notion of the incurability of mental deficiency. He experimented with what he called the 'psychological method' of training and in 1837 established the first school devoted to the education of mentally defective children; this method provided intensive training in sensory discrimination and muscular control—techniques which quickly gained universal recognition, especially in America, and which were subsequently incorporated into 'performance' or non-verbal tests of intelligence.

MENTAL TESTING AND MEASUREMENT

The influence of the early experimental psychologists

Mention must also be made of the effect on the development of the mental testing movement, of the work of the experimental psychologists in the nineteenth century. Their enquiries were not concerned with the measurement of individual differences, but aimed instead to provide generalized descriptions of human behaviour. As Anastasi (1954) has stated:

> It was the uniformities rather than the differences in behaviour which were the focus of attention. Individual differences were either ignored or were accepted as a necessary evil which limited the applicability of the generalization. Thus the fact that one individual reacted differently from another when observed under identical conditions was regarded as a form of 'error'. The presence of such error, or individual invariability rendered the generalization approximate rather than exact.

This attitude prevailed throughout the early psychological laboratories, particularly in Europe where, under the influence of Wundt, experiments were conducted not into individual differences as such, but into the general features of visual, auditory and other sensory processes, the analysis of mental associations and simple reaction time experiments.

The influence of all these experiments was that the earliest psychological tests were concerned in the main with only the simplest mental processes. Even more significant however, was the fact that early experimental investigations emphasized the need to standardize testing procedures and conditions which now constitute the

MENTAL TESTING AND MEASUREMENT

defining characterists of the good psychological test.

The contributions of Sir Francis Galton

In Britain the earliest investigations into mental testing and measurement were those conducted by Sir Francis Galton and subsequently extended by his disciple and collaborator, Karl Pearson. Indeed, Galton's visionary ideas about the nature of general and specific intellectual abilities, the use of psychological tests, the technique of correlation and the hierarchial structure of cognitive functions both initiated and provided the main impetus for the study of individual differences in this country.

One of Galton's earliest studies consisted of an experimental investigation of the associative processes in which he showed the extraordinary frequency and readiness of associations in childhood and the significance that these and the early years have generally for the development of the adult personality. Another series of experiments were carried out on mental imagery, this being the first large-scale use of the questionnaire as a psychological instrument. These enquiries, however, served but to further a more ultimate purpose in his work. As Burt (1962) has pointed out:

> They formed only a few of the practical applications of an underlying theoretical study—and it was the need for the preliminary theoretical study—a study by the most rigorous scientific techniques—which he wished chiefly to urge. The basis was to be a genuine science of the individual man. All Galton's work—the statistical contributions, his researches into heredity, his invention of rating scale and mental tests, his studies of nature

and nurture—these were merely means to his great work.

Galton's idea of devising and using mental tests for the purpose of measuring differences and intellectual ability, functions and other psychological qualities took shape at his Anthropometric Laboratory at University College, London, in the 1880s. And although his idea that tests of sensory discrimination reflected intellectual ability was a mistaken one, his work stood out as the first large-scale systematic collection of data on individual differences in the mind. Of particular importance was his abiding interest in human heredity and genius, and as early as 1869 he attempted a classification of people according to their intelligence or natural ability, the details of which are reproduced below:

Classification of Men according to their natural gifts (Galton)

Grade	I.Q.	%	Description
A	100	25.7	Mediocre
B	110	16.2	Good Average
C	120	6.3	Foreman of average jury
D	130	1.6	Obtains the ordinary prizes of life
E	140	0.2	Highly successful
F	150	0.023	Eminent ⎫ Genius
G	160	0.001	Illustrious ⎭

In this table, estimated I.Q.s have been added for illustrative purposes by Burt. The description of the several categories, however, is that provided by Galton himself.

MENTAL TESTING AND MEASUREMENT

Cattell and other early mental tests

Another prominent psychologist in the development of mental tests was the American J. McKeen Cattell who, from 1890 onwards, administered a wide variety of tests to college students in an attempt to determine their intellectual level.

The tests, which included measures of muscular strength, of vision and hearing, weight discrimination and memory, were constructed on an assumption similar to that held by Galton, namely, that intellectual functions could be inferred from tests of sensory discrimination. Cattell's preference for these latter tests was also influenced by his belief that whereas such simple mental functions could be obtained with reasonable precision, the measurement of the more complex processes of reasoning and intelligence was an impossible task. Such a belief resulted in the construction of a large number of sensory tests during the last decade of the nineteenth century—a development which brought a reaction from the French psychologists Binet and Henri who criticized the tests on the grounds that they concentrated unduly on simple specialized ability instead of on more complex functions like imagination, attention, comprehension, reasoning ability and aesthetic appreciation. Tests of the latter processes were, as we shall see, included in Binet's and Simon's own famous measures of intelligence.

Binet and the rise of intelligence tests

Binet, who founded the first psychological laboratory in France at the Sorbonne in 1889, tried out many ways of measuring intelligence (physical traits, handwriting analysis, even palmistry) and after a long series of investigations in the primary schools of Paris, constructed a scale of tests consisting of 30 problems of increasing difficulty that in Binet's (1905) own words were 'simple, rapid, convenient, precise, heterogeneous, holding the subject in continual contact with the experimentor and principally upon the faculty of judgments'.

As a result of his experiments, Binet found that the kinds of test-items that discriminated effectively between bright children and dull children did not consist of new tasks that challenged their problem-solving ability, but were tasks that were familiar, or even commonplace, e.g. distinguishing between a neatly drawn face and an untidy one, stringing square beads alternatively with round ones, naming coins, completing analogies, recognizing absurdities and so on.

These kinds of questions really ask, 'How much has the child learned, without any special training, about his environment?' 'What sort of problems has he solved for himself in his observation of common phenomena and of social relations?' In brief, Binet's tests were closely related to the children's past experience. They sampled the kinds of activities that were open, as far as possible, to all children of the culture. In other words, the tests measured those functions which were largely acquired in the course of the children's ordinary living—comprehending, reasoning, judging and general efficiency of thinking.

As Binet and his co-worker Simon (1905) stated:

It seems to us that in intelligence there is a fundamental faculty, the alteration or the lack of which, is of the utmost importance for practical life. This faculty is judgment, otherwise called good sense, practical sense, initiative, the faculty of adapting one's self to circumstances. To judge well, to comprehend well, to reason well, these are the essential activities of intelligence. A person may be a moron or an imbecile, if he is lacking in judgment; but with good judgment he can never be either. Indeed the rest of the intellectual faculties seem of little importance in comparison with judgment. What does it matter, for example whether the organs of sense function normally of what import that certain ones are hyperaesthetic, or that others are anaesthetic or are weakened?

Laura Bridgeman, Helen Keller and their fellow-unfortunates were blind as well as deaf, but this did not prevent them from being very intelligent. Certainly this is demonstrative proof that the total or even partial integrity of the senses does not form a mental factor equal to judgment. We may measure the acuteness of the sensibility of subjects; nothing could be easier. But we should do this, not so much to find out the state of their sensibility as to learn the exactitude of their judgment.

The same remark holds good for the study of the memory. At first glance, memory being a psychological phenomenon of capital importance, one would be tempted to give it a very conspicuous part in an examination of intelligence. But memory is distinct from independence of judgment. One may have good sense and lack memory. The reverse is also common. Just at the present time we are observing a backward girl who is developing before our astonished eyes a memory very much greater than our own. We have measured that memory and we are not deceived by it. Nevertheless, that girl presents a most beautifully classic type of imbecility.

As a result of all this investigation in the scale which

we present, we accord the first place to judgment; that which is of importance to us is not certain errors which the subject commits, but absurd errors, which prove that he lacks judgment.

One of the remarkable features of Binet's writings, as Rosenblith and Allensmith (1966) have indicated, is the extraordinary sophistication of his thoughts and his awareness of issues that are still all too frequently lost sight of, e.g. that schooling should always be in accordance with the natural development of children and that they should only be taught what they are sufficiently mature to understand.

The original scale of intelligence devised by Binet in 1905 was followed by the 1908 and 1911 tests and in the latter's revision, developed by L. M. Terman (1916) the Intelligence Quotient, (I.Q.) or ratio between a child's Mental Age and Chronological Age, was first used.

A further American version appeared in 1937. Meanwhile, an English standardization of the 1911 Scale was carried out by Burt in 1921 and it is interesting to note his comments on the preface regarding the importance of sound judgment as the principal means by which to assess the validity and usefulness of test results. Burt writes:

> Tests, infinitely more scientific than those set out below, can still be but the beginning, never the end, of the examination of the child. To take a young mind as it is, and delicately one by one to sound its notes and stops, to detect the smaller discords and appreciate the subtle harmonies is more of an art than a service. The scientist may standardize the method; to apply that method and to appraise the results demands the tact, the experience, the imaginative insight of the teacher born and trained.

MENTAL TESTING AND MEASUREMENT

The Binet-type tests and all their revisions are *individual* tests in that they can only be administered to one person at a time. A further characteristic of these tests is that they required highly trained examiners and as such are essentially clinical tests for the intensive study of individual cases. For these and other reasons such tests are unsuited for group administration and other measures of intelligence which could be applied to large numbers of subjects at the same time came to be developed.

Group tests

Group tests of intelligence were first introduced in America in 1917 by a Committee of the American Psychological Association under the direction of Robert M. Yerkes for the rapid classification of army recruits. Known as the Army Alpha and Beta Tests, they consisted of verbal and non-verbal scales and after World War I were released for general civilian use. They underwent many revisions and soon other group intelligence tests were being constructed for all kinds of persons, children and adults. Large-scale testing programmes were launched and though many of the tests were crude instruments, the testing movement generally underwent a tremendous spurt of growth.

Meanwhile in Britain, too, psychologists, including Spearman, McDougall, William Brown, Flugel, Thomson and Burt were all busy developing intelligence and other tests for use in schools and clinics. In 1914-15, for example, P. B. Ballard (1915, 1920, 1922, 1923, 1949) as Education Inspector of the L.C.C. first introduced standardized scales of reading and arithmetic for English children. Another pioneer was W. H. Winch (1910, 1913, 1914, 1921) who demonstrated the value of objective tests in the study of memory, reasoning, the transfer of training and other educational abilities.

Some of the more extensive investigations into children's abilities by means of standardized tests that were carried out from 1920 onwards were those of Sir Godfrey Thomson. Commencing in 1921 with experiments into the use of group tests of intelligence for the selection of pupils for secondary schools, Thomson's principal work, in addition to his contributions to colonial education and his great gifts as a teacher, were his large-scale surveys of the social and geographical distribution of intelligence, his studies of the differential birth-rate and his well-known 'sampling theory' of mental 'bonds' or powers. Sutherland (1958) has said of these studies:

> . . . most of his work in large-scale intelligence surveys developed out of a desire to give an equal educational chance to children in different classes of society and in different districts, and throughout his life he laboured unceasingly to hold open the gates of higher education to all able children no matter how humble their birth.

At the same time as Thomson's work was going on in Scotland, Burt was carrying out his own investigations of mental subnormality, delinquency and backwardness, combining these researches with factoral studies of intelligence and other mental functions. Few psychologists indeed have covered so many fields and worked with so many techniques as Burt and Thomson. It is too early yet to assess the true value of their work, but certain aspects of it clearly represent outstanding achievements. Thus both men extended and gave a more rigorous form to Spearman's statistical methods, thereby bringing a greater degree of mathematical exactitude into psychological and educational experimentation. Their work has also provided us with a better understanding of the measures of intelligence and has demonstrated the importance of a recognition of individual differences in education—not only in children's intellectual abilities and school work generally, but in the more subtle attributes of their temperaments, and personalities as well.

Theories of mental structure

Mention should also be made at this point of an important extension of the psychology of individual differences which took place at the beginning of the century. It consisted of attempts to arrive at a picture of the structure of the mind through the classification of mental abilities by statistical procedures. This was the principal problem which occupied students of individual psychology at this time.

The precise questions, as Burt (1955) has indicated, were concerned with the nature of intellectual ability. Were there, as the faculty psychologists had maintained, a number of special abilities each independent of the rest? Was there, instead, just one general capacity for intelligence? Or was there both a general ability and a number of special abilities? Or was there no discernible structure of the mind at all?

The first person to apply statistical methods to these problems was Galton who, with his collaborator, Pearson, devised a simple procedure, known as a correlation coefficient, by means of which the relationship between test results could be appraised.

Spearman's two-factor theory This technique was subsequently employed by Spearman (1923) who applied different tests to numerous children, determined the coefficients and then drew certain inferences about the abilities underlying the children's performance. He found that all the tests were positively correlated and that they could be arranged in hierarchical order, from highest to lowest. From this he concluded that there was something common to the tests and that it was due to a unitary factor of intelligence which he called 'g'—general intellectual ability. In addition to 'g' Spearman also found other abilities specific to individual tests, and he inferred from this that a child's score could accordingly be accounted for completely by a certain amount of general ability, together with an amount of specific ability relevant to the test.

Spearman's views were called the Two-Factor theory and two features of it are now thoroughly substantiated, though a third feature is wrong. Spearman was mistaken in his assumption that any testing of intellectual abilities would produce one and the same 'g'. Subsequent research has shown that this is not so and that 'g' is not something unitary. On the other hand, the fact that positive correlations exist among all abilities is clearly indicated and so is hierarchical structure. Both these features of Spearman's work show that the notion of 'g' is a tenable one, whatever its psychological nature might be.

The technique Spearman used, known as factor-analysis, led to the development of other theories of mental structure, principally Thomson's Sampling Theory, Burt's Theory of Hierarchical Structure and Thurston's Theory of Primary Mental Abilities.

All these, as Peel (1957) has pointed out, are based on

the correlations between tests and they all attempt to account for the coefficients by trying to find the common elements or ingredients in them. These are called 'factors' and determine the inter-correlations in a matrix of coefficients.

Thomson's sampling theory Spearman's view that intelligence was made up of a single, unitary power allied with more specialized abilities each of which accounted for activity in a group of similar achievements was not held by Thomson (1950), who claimed that a somewhat different theory of intelligence could account for the relationships between tests.

Thomson held that the mind was composed of many independent abilities of mental bonds and that intelligence consisted not only of a general factor (g) but also overlapping groups of factors which were common to some tests but not others. Typical among these group factors were verbal ability, number ability, spatial ability, speed and so on. In addition, there were also specific factors (s) particular to certain tests. In other words, Thomson believed that all tests partake of 'g' (general intellectual ability) and some tests, but not all, have different group factors.

This theory is much more adequate than Spearman's for it not only accounts for the fact of hierarchy and the inter-correlations, but also, as Peel (1957) has indicated, it helps to explain why abilities in different school subjects depend not merely on 'g' but on group-factors of various kinds.

Burt's theory of hierarchical structure

General intelligence-integrative capacity

R_1 R_2

relation finding and applying
(cognitive and aesthetic)

finding   applying

M memory   Association   H habit formation

P perception   C co-ordinated movement

Sensori-motor level
sensation and simple movements.

P   M   S   M   P   C   H   H   C

The theory of mental structure outlined by Thomson was shared in its main aspects by Burt. In his scheme, all kinds of mental are provided for and these become differentiated through maturation learning and experience. In this, Burt conforms to the evolutionary doctrine of infinite and progressive variation and integration that had been proposed earlier by Spencer, Darwin and Galton.

The mental processes described by Burt consisted, firstly, of simple sensations, movements, and other reactions (Sensori-Motor Level). This was followed by more complicated processes of perception and co-ordinated movement (called the Perceptual-Movement Level), and this, in turn, was followed at the Associative Level, by the functions of memory, habit, vocabulary, visual and auditory imagery. Finally, at the Relation-Finding Level, there appeared the processes of abstraction, generalization and formal thought.

Burt called intelligence the 'integrative capacity of mind', and maintained that this showed itself at every level but differed both in kind and degree.

The expression 'integrative capacity', is similar to the term 'apperception' which was used by Leibnitz to denote attention and adapted by Herbart (1816) to refer to the totality of conscious activities that are involved in the choice and interpretation of a given sensory element. In a broad sense, 'apperception' or 'integrative capacity' mean the sum of all former experiences—either sensory or reflective—which is involved when one gives meaning to anything.

Thurstone's primary mental abilities Another theory, quite different from the traditional British view of Thomson and Burt concerning general and group factors, was put forward by Thurstone. He found no evidence for a general factor underlying mental ability and claimed to have isolated, by factorial analysis, several basic, group factors. These were V (Verbal Ability), W (Word Fluency), N (Number), S (Spatial Ability), M (Memory) P (Perceptual Speed) and R (Reasoning).

The Reasoning Factor described by Thurstone consisted of what he called I (Induction) and D (Deduction). In later studies, however, the Deduction Factor disappeared and Induction was named Reasoning.

In commenting on the differences between British and American views Vernon (1961) has stated:

> British writers make 'g' as large as possible and group factors only when the residuals necessitate them, whereas Americans either introduce 'g' as a second-order factor, or, if a primary one is unavoidable, tend to minimize it. Again, British workers recognize large or more comprehensive group factors together with sub-factors, 'descended' from them, whereas American primary factors after all possess much the same status and variance. Not only do such primary factors seem, from our standpoint, to carry some of the variance that would be better attributed to 'g' but also one or more of them (usually a reasoning factor) may consist wholly as 'g'.

Some further comments have been made by Vernon (1961) concerning factorial theories generally, and the first concerns the number of factors that may account for the inter-correlations of any battery of tests. The fact that one can assume a general factor, as Spearman did, or a general factor along with other group factors, as Thomson and Burt did, or dispense with a general factor altogether, as Thurstone did, shows that one's views of mental structure depends entirely on what one wishes to find out. In addition, the estimation of the factors themselves depends on the nature of the tests and the sample and the method of analysis that is used. If these change, the factors change.

Another point mentioned by Vernon concerns the psychological reality of the factors. In some respects Thomson tended to regard them as 'statistical artefacts' though he also believed that they could come to have a real existence in the sense of being practically useful. For Burt, factors were 'descriptive categories' and more meaningful. Whatever view is adopted, these theories of mental structure have shown one thing quite clearly and it is that intelligence, whatever its nature, is not a unitary type of ability but, in Vernon's words, 'a very fluid collection of overlapping abilities, comprising the whole of mental life'.

The value and limitations of mental tests

In summarizing the development of mental tests over the past 100 years, it will be noted that the earliest experimental work was limited to the simplest psychological processes—to sense discrimination, muscular control and elementary mental associations. These enquiries were followed by the contributions of Galton, Cattell, Seguin and particularly Binet and his co-workers, all of whom constructed tests of intellectual performance and emphasized both the need to standardize testing procedures and to arrive at age-norms of performance.

The development of the group testing movement, both in Britain and America, extended mental testing still further with the result that there is now a wide variety of

MENTAL TESTING AND MEASUREMENT

standardized measures available, not only in intelligence and all the basic educational skills, but in the social and emotional aspects of behaviour as well.

The value and limitations of these tests are dependent on how well they have been constructed and standardized, i.e. on how valid, reliable and objective they are, and how useful they are in helping teachers and others to make decisions about an individual child or group. In practical terms, standardized tests are valuable in compiling school and class records, in estimating progress and in discovering individual differences and difficulties. They are thus an aid in helping teachers make predictions about children's behaviour with reasonable accuracy and objectivity.

Although adequately standardized tests usually gives assessments which are quite valid and reliable, they are not perfect measuring instruments, and if no allowances are made for individual fluctuations, they can label children and even, at times, place a stigma on their ability. Again, if used slavishly, tests can dominate the life of a school and restrict the freedom of the curriculum. In addition, too frequent application renders them less effective, especially if they are used as teaching material. Finally, they are liable to misinterpretation unless handled carefully. Considerable skill and experience are necessary, especially in using individual tests. The good tester, therefore, tends to be cautious in his interpretation of test results. He cannot afford to be dogmatic because he is only too conscious of the possible influence of many unknown factors.

When used sensibly, however, mental tests are important tools in education. They act as a check on one's own personal judgment and while there will probably always be problems connected with their use and interpretation, they are not incapable of logical justification or scientific refinement and, as such, constitute one of the most valuable developments of modern educational psychology.

Further reading

1. *Books dealing with the history of psychology*

HEARNSHAW, L. S. (1964) *A Short History of British Psychology*, Methuen.
 A comprehensive account of the development of psychology in Great Britain over the past 100 years. The influence of evolutionary theory and the contributions of Galton, McDougall, Spearman, Burt and the early child psychologists are carefully assessed in relation to concomitant social, scientific and intellectual developments.

BRETT, G. S. (1962) *History of Psychology*, edited and abridged by R. S. Peters, Allen & Unwin.
 An informed summary of Professor Brett's three classic volumes. The sections dealing with the rationalist and observationalist traditions are particularly useful and so are the accounts of nineteenth-century influences of biology and physiology. Twentieth-century trends are also outlined.

MURPHY, G. (1960) *An Historical Introduction to Modern Psychology*, Routledge & Kegan Paul.
 Excellent summaries are provided of the development of experimental psychology and of the other major psychological systems, including the rise of the mental testing movement, child psychology and personality theory.

KNIGHT, M. (1954) *William James*, Penguin.
 A lucid commentary on James' psychological writings compiled, with readings, from the 'Principles' and the 'Briefer Course'. The

sections dealing with his treatment of habit and attention and his views on interest and effort in education are particularly useful.

2. Books dealing with child psychology

BREARLEY, M. and HITCHFIELD, E. (1966) *A Teacher's Guide to Reading Piaget*, Routledge & Kegan Paul.

A book of practical value. It explains the complex theoretical ideas of Piaget concerning the development of the child's concepts of number, measurement and other forms of logical thought.

LAWRENCE, E. (1952) *Friedrich Froebel and English Education*, U.L.P.

An evaluation of the Froebel movement in Britain, with particular reference to the origin of the kindergarten and his influence on primary schools today. Froebel's educational philosophy is also discussed in relation to modern psychological knowledge.

GESELL, A. (1940) *The First Five Years*, Harper.

A psychological outline, from the point of view of a hereditarian, of child development from birth to the fifth year.

ISAACS, S. (1951) *Social Development in Young Children*, edited by Dorothy May, Routledge & Kegan Paul.

An abridged edition of one of Isaacs' classics in which a large body of psychological material illustrative of the young child's unconscious attitudes and early conflicts are interpreted in terms of modern psychoanalytic theory.

HEAFFORD, M. R. (1961) *Pestalozzi*, Methuen.

A critical account of Pestalozzi's most important educational ideas. Certain features of his theories are given special consideration, namely, his views on intellectual and moral education, discipline and the role of teachers and parents.

PIAGET, J. (1967) *The Psychology of Intelligence*, Routledge & Kegan Paul.

A presentation of the main theories of intelligence and an account of Piaget's own view, based on the formation of operations.

ROSENBLITH, J. F., and ALLINSMITH, W. (1966) *The Causes of Behaviour*, Allyn and Bacon.

FURTHER READING

A book of readings and commentaries by important theorists or schools of thought about developmental psychology. The final section deals with research and problems of specific implication to learning and teaching.

3. Books dealing with theories of learning

BIGGE, M. L. (1964) *Learning Theories for Teachers*, Harper.
A good basic text which describes, semi-historically and comparatively, the principal modern theories and their relation to teaching.

HILL, WINIFRED F. (1963) *Learning*, Methuen.
An elementary but most useful account of modern learning theories and their implications for the classroom.

KLAUSEMEIR, H. J. (1964) *Learning and Human Abilities*, Harper.
An up-to-date text which applies the findings of modern psychological research to the development of a theory of classroom learning. Attention is also given to contemporary teaching methods, including television, teaching machines and team-teaching.

4. Books dealing with mental testing and measurement

BURT, C. (1962) *Mental and Scholastic Tests*, 4th ed, Staples.
This edition contains a systematic account of the value and limitations of standardized tests of intelligence and attainment. Recent views on the nature of general ability and specific aptitudes and the statistical procedures that are used in the analysis of test data are included in the revised appendicies.

CRONBACH, L. J. (1960) *Essentials of Psychological Testing*, Harper.
This authoritative book outlines the basic concepts of psychological testing in education, counselling and guidance. The principal kinds of tests in the fields of general ability and personality assessment are carefully described and useful computing guides are provided.

GULLIKSEN, H. (1967) *Theory of Mental Tests*, 6th ed, Wiley.
A sophisticated text for students interested in the statistical procedures underlying test construction. Useful methods of constructing and standardizing test items and of estimating

FURTHER READING

errors of measurement are given. Although the book is written primarily for those engaged in test development, many of the techniques are applicable to other areas, such as the measurement of attitude and opinions and the appraisal of personality.

VERNON, P. E. (1961) *The Structure of Human Abilities*, Methuen. A condensed guide to the measurement of mental abilities and modern methods of factorial analysis. Summarizes many research studies, British and American, and provides definite conclusions on controversial issues.

Bibliography

ADLER, A. (1935) *The Education of Children*, translated by Eleanor and Friedrich Jensen. Allen & Unwin. (1958) *The Individual Psychology of Alfred Adler*, edited by Ansbacher. Allen & Unwin.
ALLEN, R. M. (1958) *Personality Assessment Procedures*. New York: Harper.
ALLPORT, G. W. (1937) *Personality: A Psychological Interpretation*. New York: Holt.
ANASTASI, A. (1954) *Psychological Testing*. New York: Macmillan.
ANDERSON, H. (1945-6) Studies of Teachers' Classroom Personalities. In *Appl. Psychol. Monogr*. Nos 6, 8, 11.
ARISTOTLE (1954) *'De Anima' in the version of William of Moerbeke and the Commentary of St Thomas Aquinas*. Routledge & Kegan Paul.

BAIN, A. (1859) *The Emotions and the Will*. Parker & Son (1874) *Mind and Body*. Kegan Paul.
BALLARD, P. B. (1949) *Group Tests of Intelligence*. University of London Press.
BARTLETT, F. (1950) *Remembering*. Cambridge Psychological Laboratory.
BEKHTEREV (1913) *La Psychologie Objective*. Alcan. (1932) *General Principles of Human Reflexology*. International.
BENEDICT, R. (1935) *Patterns of Culture*. Routledge & Kegan Paul.
BERLYNE, D. E. (Feb. 1957) Recent Developments in Piaget's Work. In *B. J. Ed. Psych*. Vol. 27.

BIBLIOGRAPHY

BINET, A. (1905 & 1908) *L'Année Psychologique* Vols XI & XIV.
BRADLEY, F. H. (1935) *Collected Essays*. Oxford University Press.
BRETT, G. S. (1962) *History of Psychology*, edited by R. S. Peters. Allen & Unwin.
BUROS, O. K. (1959) *The Fifth Mental Measurements Year Book*. New Jersey: Gryphon Press.
BURT, C. (1949) The Structure of the Mind, Parts I & II. In *B. J. Ed. Psych.* (1938) *The Young Delinquent*, 4th edition. University of London Press. (1962) *Mental and Scholastic Tests*. Staples Press. (1955) Evidence for the Concept of Intelligence. In *B. J. Ed. Psych.*

CAJAL, R. S. (1959) *Degeneration and Regeneration of the Nervous System*, translated by Raoul M. May. New York: Hafner.
CATTELL, R. B. (1946) *Description and Measurement of Personality*. New York: World Book Co. (1950) *An Introduction to Personality Study*. Hutchinson. (1957) *Personality and Motivation Structure and Measurement*. Harrap.
CLAPAREDE, E. (1912) J. J. Rousseau et la conception fonctionelle de l'enfance. In *Revue de Metaphysique et de Morale*, 20.

DARWIN, C. (1859) *The Origin of Species*. Murray.

EBBINGHAUS, H. (1885) *Memory*, translated by H. A. Ruger and C. E. Bussenius. Columbia.
ERIKSON, E. (1951) *Childhood and Society*. Imago Publications.
EVANS, K. M. (1961) *Sociometry and Education*. Routledge & Kegan Paul.
EYSENCK, H. J. (1960) *The Structure of Human Personality*, 2nd edition. Methuen. (1957) *The Dynamics of Anxiety and Hysteria*. Routledge & Kegan Paul. (Feb. 1960) The Development of Moral Values in Children. In *B. J. Ed. Psych.* 30, i, pp. ii-22.

FAIRBAIRN, R. (1952) *Psycho-analytic Studies of the Personality*. Tavistock.
FLEMING, C. (1958) The Child Within the Group. In *Studies in Education* No 7. Evans.
FLETCHER, R. (1957) *Instinct in Man*. Allen & Unwin.
FLUGEL, J. C. (1953) *A Hundred Years of Psychology, 1833-1933*. Duckworth.
FREUD, ANNA (1937) *The Ego and the Mechanisms of Defence*.

BIBLIOGRAPHY

Hogarth. (1952) *The Psychoanalytic Study of the Child*. Imago Publications.
FREUD, S. (1914) *Psychopathology of Everyday Life*. Unwin. (1915) *The Unconscious*. In *Collected Papers* Vol IV. (1927) *The Future of an Illusion*. Hogarth Press. (1930) *Civilization and its Discontents*. Hogarth Press.
FROEBEL, F. (1826) *The Education of Man*. (1967) *Friedrich Froebel: A Selection from his Writings*, by Irene M. Lilley. Cambridge University Press.

GALTON, F. (1896) *Hereditary Genius*. Macmillan. (1883) *Inquiries into Human Faculty and its Measurement*. Macmillan.
GESSELL, A. (1928) *Infancy and Human Growth*. New York: Macmillan. (1934) *An Atlas of Infant Behaviour* 2 vols. New Haven: Yale University Press. (1934) Growth Potential and Infant Personality. In *Infant Behaviour*. McGraw Hill. (1940) *Development Diagnosis*. New York: Hoeber. (1944) *Infant and Child in the Culture of Today*. Hamilton.
GREEN, T. H. (1883) *Prolegomena to Ethics*. Oxford Warehouse. (1885-8) *Collected Works* 3 vols. Longmans.

HEARNSHAW, L. S. (1964) *Short History of Modern Psychology, 1840-1940*. Methuen. (1964) *Short History of British Psychology, 1840-1940*. Methuen.
HERBART (1816) *Outlines of Psychology*.
HILL, W. F. (1963) *Learning* Methuen.
H.M.S.O. (1931) *Hadow Report*.

ISAACS, S. (1930) *Intellectual Growth in Young Children*. Routledge & Kegan Paul, (1932) *The Children We Teach*. University of London Press. (1933) *Social Development in Young Children*. Routledge & Kegan Paul.

JAMES, W. (1892) *Principles of Psychology: Briefer Course*. Macmillan.
JONES, E. (1953-5) *Sigmund Freud: Life and Work*. Hogarth Press.
JUDD, C. H. (1908) The Relation of Special Training and General Intelligence. In *Educ. Review* 36.
JUNG, C. C. (1921) *The Psychology of the Unconscious*. Kegan Paul. (1953) *Psychological Reflections*. Routledge & Kegan. (1953)

BIBLIOGRAPHY

Two Essays on Analytical Psychology. Routledge & Kegan Paul. (1954) *The Development of Personality.* Routledge & Kegan Paul.

KESSEN, W. (1965) *The Child.* New York: Wiley.
KLEIN, J. (1948) *The Study of Groups.* Routledge & Kegan Paul.
KNIGHT, R. (1958) Children's Needs and Interests. In *Studies in Education* No 7. Evans.
KOHLER, W. (1927) *The Mentality of Apes.* Kegan Paul.
KOFFKA, K. (1924) *The Growth of the Mind.* Kegan Paul.

LEIBNITZ, G. W. (1934) *Philosophical Writings*, translated by Mary Morris. Dent.
LEWIN, K. (1936) *Principles of Topological Psychology*, translated by Fritz and Grace Heider. New York: McGraw-Hill. (1954) *Modern Learning Theory.* New York: Appleton Century Crofts.
LORENZ, K. (1952) *King Solomon's Ring.* Methuen.
LYNN, R. (1960) Two Personality Characteristics Related to Academic Achievement. In *B. J. Ed. Psych.* Vol. 29, pp. 213-6. (1960) The Relation of Neuroticism and Extraversion to Intelligence Attainment. In *B. J. Ed. Psych.* Vol. 31, Part II, pp. 194-203.

MCDOUGALL, W. (1936) *An Introduction to Social Psychology*, 23rd edition. Methuen.
MEAD, M. (1955) *Childhood in Contemporary Cultures.* University of Chicago Press.
MORENO, J. L. (1954) *Who Shall Survive?* Washington: Nervous and Mental Disease Publishing Co.
MORRIS, B. (1958) Mental Health in the Classroom. In *Studies in Education* No. 7. Evans.
MURPHY, G. (1949) *An Historical Introduction to Modern Psychology*, 5th edition. Routledge & Kegan Paul.

NOTT, K. (28 January 1962) Underworld and Unconscious. In the *Sunday Times.*
NUNN, P. (1945) *Education: its Data and First Principles*, 3rd edition. Arnold.

PAVLOV, I. P. (1928) *Conditioned Reflexes: an Investigation of the Physiological Activity of the Cerebral Cortex*, translated by G. V. Anrep. Oxford University Press.

BIBLIOGRAPHY

PEEL, E. A. (1957) *The Psychological Basis of Education*. Edinburgh: Oliver & Boyd.

PESTALOZZI, J. H. (1894) *How Gertrude Teaches her Children*. Syracuse, New York: Bardeen.

PETERS, R. S. (1962) *Brett's History of Psychology*, Allen & Unwin.

PIAGET, J. (1924) *Language and Thought of the Child*. Kegan Paul. (1929) *The Child's Conception of Physical Causality*. Kegan Paul. (1947) *The Psychology of Intelligence*. Routledge & Kegan Paul.

PREYER, W. T. (1889) *The Mind of the Child*. Appleton.

QUICK, R. H. (1895) *Essays on Educational Reformers*. Longmans Green.

ROGERS, C. H. (1942) *Counselling and Psychotherapy*. Boston: Houghton Mifflin.

ROSENBLITH, J. F. (1966) *The Causes of Behaviour, II*. Boston: Allyn & Bacon.

ROUSSEAU, J.-J. (1911) *Émile, or On Education*, translated by Barbara Foxley. Dent.

RUSK, R. (1954) *Doctrines of the Great Educators*. Macmillan.

SHERRINGHAM, C. S. (1906) *The Integrative Action of the Nervous System*. Constable.

SPEARMAN, C. (1923) *The Nature of Intelligence and the Principles of Cognition*. Macmillan.

SPENCER, H. (1855 & 1872) *Principles of Psychology*, 2 vols. Williams & Norgate. (1852) *Developmental Hypotheosis*. (1896) *Education: Intellectual, Moral and Physical*.

SPROTT, W. (1958) *Human Groups*. Penguin.

STEWART, M. (1962) *Sociology of Education*. Routledge & Kegan Paul.

SULLY, J. (1894) *The Teacher's Handbook of Psychology*. On the basis of *Outlines of Psychology*. Longmans. (1895) *Studies of Childhood*. Longmans. (1897) *Children's Ways*. Longmans. (1902) *An Essay on Laughter*. Longmans.

SUTHERLAND, J. D. (1958) *Psycho-analysis and Contemporary Thought*. Hogarth Press.

TERMAN, LEWIS M. (1937) *Measuring Intelligence*. Harrap.

THOMSON, G. (1950) *The Factoral Analysis of Human Ability*. University of London Press.

BIBLIOGRAPHY

THORNDIKE, E. L. (1906) *Elements of Psychology*. Kegan Paul. (1906) *The Principles of Teaching*. Kegan Paul (1910) *Educational Psychology*. Kegan Paul.

THORPE, J. G. (May 1960) Neuroticism in Children. In *B. J. Psychology* Vol. 51, Part II, pp. 11-21.

THURSTONE, L. L. (1937) *Primary Mental Abilities*. Chicago.

TINBERGEN, N. (1951) *The Study of Instinct*. Oxford: Clarendon Press.

VERNON, P. E. (1956) *The Measurement of Abilities*. University of London Press. (1957) *Personality Tests and Assessments*. Methuen. (1961) *The Structure of Human Abilities*. Methuen.

WALDEYER (1891) *Deutsch. Med. Wochenschr.*

WARBURTON, F. (1962) *The Measurement of Personality* Parts I & II. In *Educational Research* Vol. IV, Nos. 1-2.

WARD, J. (1886) Psychology. In *Encyclopaedia Britannica* 9th edition.

WATSON, J. B. (1928) *Psychological Care Of Infant and Child*. New York: Norton.

WERTHEIMER, M. (1961) *Productive Thinking*. Tavistock.

WINCH, W. H. (1913) *Child Study*.

WOODWORTH, R. S. (1901) The Influence of Improvement in One Mental Function upon the Efficiency of Other Functions. In *Psychol. Review* 8.